Not
Your Mother's®
Slow Cooker
Family
Favorites

Also by Beth Hensperger

Not Your Mother's Weeknight Cooking

Not Your Mother's Slow Cooker Recipes for Two

The Gourmet Potluck

The Bread Lover's Bread Machine Cookbook

The Best Quick Breads

Bread for Breakfast

Bread Made Easy

The Pleasure of Whole Grain Breads

The Bread Bible

Breads of the Southwest

Beth's Basic Bread Book

Bread for All Seasons

Baking Bread

Bread

Also by Beth Hensperger and Julie Kaufmann

Not Your Mother's Slow Cooker Recipes for Entertaining

Not Your Mother's Slow Cooker Cookbook

The Ultimate Rice Cooker Cookbook

Not Your Mother's® Slow Cooker Family Favorites

Beth Hensperger

The Harvard Common Press
Boston, Massachusetts

THE HARVARD COMMON PRESS
535 Albany Street
Boston, Massachusetts 02118
www.harvardcommonpress.com

Printed in the United States of America
Printed on acid-free paper

Library of Congress Cataloging-in-Publication Data

Hensperger, Beth.
  Not your mother's slow cooker family favorites / Beth Hensperger.
    p. cm.
  Includes index.
  ISBN 978-1-55832-409-1 (pbk.)—ISBN 978-1-55832-408-4 (hardcover)
    1. Electric cookery, Slow. I. Title.
  TX827.H39143 2009
  641.5'884—dc22   2008055566

Special bulk-order discounts are available on this and other Harvard Common Press books.
Companies and organizations may purchase books for premiums or resale, or may arrange
a custom edition, by contacting the Marketing Director at the address above.

Cover recipe: Lynn's Flank Steak Tostadas with Cilantro Yogurt Sauce, page 65.
Spine recipe: Apricot-Ginger Chicken Legs, page 145. Back cover recipes: Mini Turkey Meatball
Sliders, page 71; "Brinner" Cinnamon French Toast Casserole, page 38.

Book design by Ralph Fowler / rlf design
Cover photographs by Eskite Photography
Food styling by Andrea Lucich
Prop styling by Kerrie Sherrell Walsh

10 9 8 7 6 5 4 3 2 1

For my family:
Mom; Meg, Don, Nicolas, and Stefan;
Amy and Joel; Jenny, Jeremy, Courtney,
and Cooper; and Bro Jim

Acknowledgments

This book has been written in collaboration with my sister, Meg Hensperger Rohacek. Her contributions and insights made the writing of this book a joy.

Special thank-yous to Edith Wine, senior product manager at Hamilton Beach, and Rob Sheard, brand director at Breville USA.

Contents

Introduction

There has never been a countertop appliance better able to create an amazing meal with minimum muss and fuss than the slow cooker. But the challenge for time-pressed moms and dads is to come up with appealing and delicious recipes for every night of the week. *Not Your Mother's Slow Cooker Family Favorites* is here to help, with more than 100 recipes for whatever you're hungry for.

Food doesn't have to be fancy to be good—it just needs to be tasty and nourish the body and soul with warm, inviting flavor. This collection of family favorites for the slow cooker heads back to our American cooking roots, with homey soups and one-pot meals, as well as some imaginative twists on familiar recipes, all prepared with fresh ingredients.

You will find in these pages not only pot roast, poultry, and chili recipes, for which the slow cooker is famous, but casseroles, vegetable stews, soups, sandwiches, main dish salads, and a bevy of fine sauces for pasta—all developed with your comfort and ease of preparation in mind. Please feel free to modify the recipes to suit your own individual preferences.

Happy slow-cooking!

Slow-Cooking 101

The slow cooker, with its even, low heat sealed in a covered pot, uses the moisture created within the pot to cook food. It's a cooking technique that is tailor-made for foods that are not naturally tender, such as meat with a lot of connective tissue and beans and other plants with lots of fiber, transforming them into tender, delectable morsels.

It is important to understand the way a slow cooker works. The new machines are a great improvement over those sold even five years ago, so consider upgrading from your mom's hand-me-down or the one you picked up at a tag sale. If you cook a lot, consider buying a second or third machine that's a different size from the one you already have (you won't regret it).

The slow cooker's low-wattage, wrap-around heating coils are sandwiched between the inner and outer metal walls of the slow cooker to provide indirect heat; the heat source never makes direct contact with the stoneware crock. The coils inside the walls heat up, thereby heating up the space between the base wall and the crock and transferring that heat to the stoneware. There is one type of slow cooker known as an intermittent cooker, which has the heating element in the base; the recipes in this book were not tested using this type of machine.

Slow Cooker Sizes

The slow cooker is available in a wide range of volume capacities, from 1 quart to 7 1/2 quarts, increasing in 2-cup increments. It is up to you to decide what size you need, depending on the number of people you want to serve and what types of foods you are making. For family meals, I suggest a large 6-quart oval model and, if you use the appliance a lot, I recommend you also have two or three machines of other sizes, such as a 1 1/2-quart model (for making cranberry sauce, dips, and overnight oatmeal, for example), a 5-quart round (for chilis or stews), and a medium-size 3 1/2- to 4-quart pot (for casseroles, pork or turkey tenderloins, vegetables, or a big communal batch of morning cereal).

The recipes in this book recommend which size slow cooker to use for each recipe—small, medium, or large—and a preferred shape. Most every size comes in a choice of round or oval, but be sure to check inside the box when purchasing; I have found that the picture on the outside of the box often does not reflect the shape of the cooker within. Some manufacturers now make a rectangular-shaped slow cooker in large sizes. The oval is my favorite for the widest range of cooking.

When "small" is indicated in a recipe, you can use the 1 1/2- to 3-quart slow cooker. The small size is handy if you're cooking for one or two people.

Medium-size slow cookers are the 3- to 4 1/2-quart models. These are the most popular, as they are easy to handle and comfortable to lift, and they fit nicely on the counter or in the dishwasher. This size holds enough for 4 to 6 servings. It is also a good size if you're cooking for two people and you'd like to have leftovers.

Large cookers generally have a 5- to 7-quart capacity. The most popular is the 6-quart size. It is designed for families and entertaining and works best for large cuts of meat like brisket and corned beef, pot roast, whole poultry, and large-quantity stews like beef bourguignon.

If you are multiplying up a recipe created for a medium-size cooker, increase the cooking time by 1 1/2 to 2 hours and increase your ingredients by one-half or double them, depending on whether you are using a 5-, 6-, or 7-quart cooker.

The features of the different slow cookers vary along with their sizes, so take some time to consider what you will be using your crock for and buy accordingly. While most models are delightfully affordable (under $50), the new digital models are pricier. Tell your friends and family that slow cookers make fabulous gifts!

Slow Cooker Tips for Success

Please be sure to read this section before your first slow-cooking forays and use it as a reference guide thereafter.

- The cord on the slow cooker is deliberately short to minimize danger from tangling or tripping. You can use a heavy-duty extension cord only if it has a marked electrical rating at least as great as the electrical rating of your cooker.

- The manufacturer's directions will specify whether the stoneware insert, if removable, is ovenproof, microwave-safe, or able to go under the broiler.

- While some crockery inserts are oven-proof, most cannot be used on a gas or electric stovetop, as they will break if they come in direct contact with a heating element (as will any ceramic dish). (There are a few slow cookers whose crocks are specifically designed for this task.) Therefore, any time a recipe calls for browning ingredients, such as searing meat, you will generally do so first in a sauté pan, skillet, or saucepan, then transfer the food to the crock.

- Don't ever subject the stoneware insert to sudden changes in temperature, like pouring cold water into it while still hot from the cooking cycle; this can cause cracks in the insert. Be sure to let the crock come to room temperature before washing. Never store the stoneware crock in the freezer. The crock can also crack if you add a lot of frozen food to it. If your crock becomes cracked or deeply scratched, contact the manufacturer for replacement instructions. The crock should be washed by hand with non-abrasive dish-washing soap and a nylon scrubbie or brush, or placed in the dish-washer. Do not submerge the metal housing in water.

- Never preheat the crockery insert when empty. Load the crock with the ingredients, then turn on the cooker or plug it in to start the heating process.

- Never immerse the metal housing, or base, of the slow cooker in water or fill it with liquid; you must always have the crockery insert in place to cook. To clean, let the base come to room temperature, then wipe it inside and out with a damp, soapy sponge and dry with a towel so as not to damage the finish. Make sure the bottom is clean inside and free of food particles or spillage.

- For easy cleanup, coat the inside of the crock with nonstick cooking spray or use a plastic liner designed for cooking in the slow cooker.

- The glass lid of the slow cooker becomes quite hot during the cooking process.

Use a potholder to remove it, if necessary, and handle with care to avoid burns. The lid is dishwasher-safe. Keeping the lid in place during cooking is essential for proper cooking of the contents.

- Liquid quantities vary drastically in the recipes, from a few tablespoons to submerging the food completely in liquid for braising. Each recipe will be specific on these points. Ideally, the crockery insert should be filled at least half full, and no fuller than 1 inch from the rim. The best practice is to fill the insert one-half to three-quarters full; this will give you the most even cooking.

- Browning meat on the stovetop before adding it to your slow cooker can give your dish a better taste and color, as well as cut down on fat. Draining the meat and/or patting it dry before adding it to the crock can help make the dish more healthful.

- When the food is ready, if you are not serving directly out of the cooker, use heavy oven mitts to lift the hot crock carefully from its base and set it on a trivet or folded towel.

•• Adapting Conventional Recipes to the Slow Cooker ••

Once you start using the slow cooker, you will eventually want to convert some of your oven and stovetop recipes so you can prepare them in your cooker. To do so, find a recipe in this book that is similar to your recipe, such as one for pot roast or meatloaf, and follow the instructions. Remember to reduce the liquid in the conventional recipe as necessary and allow plenty of cooking time.

Use this conversion chart as a guide for translating traditional cooking times into slow cooker time. All times are approximate and, when making a recipe for the first time, be sure to check for doneness both halfway through and near the end of the cook time. Make notes on the actual cook time for future reference. Note: One hour of cooking on the HIGH setting is equal to about 2½ hours on LOW.

Conventional Recipe Time	Slow Cooker Time on LOW
15 minutes	1½ to 2 hours
20 minutes	2 to 3 hours
30 minutes	3 to 4 hours
45 minutes	5 to 6 hours
1 hour	6 to 8 hours
1½ hours	8 to 9 hours
2 hours	9 to 10 hours
3 hours	12 hours plus

•• High-Altitude Slow-Cooking ••

While it is very difficult to overcook food in the slow cooker when set on LOW, there are guidelines for slow-cooking at altitudes of more than 3,000 feet above sea level. Just remember that the higher you go, the less compressed the air is; as a result, liquids will boil at lower temperatures, and foods will take longer to cook. Figure your food will take approximately 25 percent more time to come up to the proper cooking temperature and to cook.

Just as oven temperatures need to be increased to compensate for slower heating at high altitudes, the slow cooker will run at a lower overall temperature at higher altitudes, so cook all foods on HIGH and increase the cooking time slightly. Use the LOW heat setting rather than the KEEP WARM setting for keeping food warm.

Use the following chart as a guideline. Be sure to take notes on the adjustments you make to recipes for future reference.

Adjustment	Altitude		
Cook all recipes on HIGH	3,000 feet	5,000 feet	7,000 to 8,000 feet
For each cup of liquid specified in the recipe, decrease by:	1 to 2 tablespoons	2 to 3 tablespoons	3 to 4 tablespoons

Tips on Slow Cooker Cook Times

○ You have the choice of cooking on the HIGH or LOW setting. The LOW setting is best for extended cooking, which fits into workday schedules. To cook more quickly, switch to HIGH and cook for half the time designated for cooking on the LOW setting.

○ I have found that the new slow cookers are much more efficient and run at slightly higher temperatures than older cookers. Check the wattage of your unit; there are slight differences among manufacturers. Some recipes turn out better on LOW, with its gentle, rolling simmer, than at the vigorous simmer on HIGH. Many cooks start their cookers on HIGH for about an hour to get it up to temperature, then switch to LOW for the remainder of the cooking time. Each recipe in this book specifies the best temperature setting (when appropriate) for the best results.

○ Check the food for doneness at least once toward the middle of the cook time, then again around the minimum time suggested, especially the first time you make a dish.

- Tender vegetables, noodles, and pasta overcook easily, so add them during the last 30 to 60 minutes of cooking. The same goes for seafood; add it 15 to 20 minutes before the end of cooking.

- At the end of the cooking time, remove the lid and stir the food well with a wooden or plastic spoon to prevent chipping the crock. If your dish is not cooked to your preference, replace the lid, set the cooker to HIGH, and cook further in increments of 30 to 60 minutes until the food is done to your liking. Don't worry if the dish takes longer than the recipe says; there are many variables among machines and the temperature of the ingredients that can affect the cook time.

- Once the dish is completely cooked, you can keep the food hot by switching to the LOW or KEEP WARM setting. Food can be held safely on either of these settings for up to 2 hours before eating. Many digital cookers switch automatically to the KEEP WARM setting when the cooking time is up. Do not use the KEEP WARM setting for cooking; the temperature is too low to cook foods safely.

- When your food is cooked and ready to be served, turn the machine to the OFF setting and/or unplug the unit. Many older slow cookers and smaller units do not have an OFF setting; off is when the unit is unplugged. The stoneware crock will retain heat, keeping the food warm, for a full hour after the machine is turned off.

Food Safety and the Slow Cooker

- All meat and poultry dishes must cook for a minimum of 3 hours to cook thoroughly. Do not eat undercooked food.

- Transfer leftovers to proper refrigerator or freezer storage containers within 2 hours after finishing cooking. Do not refrigerate your cooked food in the crockery insert, as the change in temperature can cause it to crack.

- Cold cooked food should not be reheated in the crockery insert as it will not reach a safe internal temperature quickly enough to render the food safe to eat. However, cooked food can be heated on the stove or in a microwave and then put into a preheated slow cooker to keep it hot until serving. To preheat the crockery insert, fill it with warm, not boiling, water and let it stand for a few minutes. Pour out the water and dry the insert, then add the food and turn on the machine to LOW.

Ingredient Tips for the Slow Cooker

- You can prep your ingredients the day before cooking: Chop vegetables and store them separately in sealed containers or plastic storage bags. Cover cut potatoes with water to prevent discoloring. Ground meat can be browned and refrigerated overnight as long as it is fully cooked (browned roasts, cubed meat, and poultry all need to be prepped just before cooking for safety since they are not fully cooked).

- Ingredients, except for meat and poultry, can be assembled in the crock, covered, and refrigerated overnight; in the morning, just place the crock into the metal housing and turn on the machine.

Vegetables

- Hard, heavier vegetables (such as carrots, winter squash, potatoes, turnips, and onions) take longer to cook than meat, so place them in the bottom of the crock and set meat or poultry on top.

- Unskinned potatoes keep their shape better in the slow cooker than peeled potatoes.

- Smaller pieces cook faster than larger chunks and whole potatoes, so for even cooking, cut all vegetables into uniform bite-size pieces.

- Lighter vegetables (such as corn, peas, and summer squash) can be layered on top or added halfway through the cooking time.

- Strong-flavored vegetables like cauliflower and broccoli, and leafy greens, are best added toward the end of cooking so as not to flavor the entire pot, unless otherwise noted.

Liquids

- In recipes for the slow cooker, you will usually use about half the recommended amount of liquid specified in a traditional stovetop or oven recipe; the condensation under the lid adds an extra $1/2$ to 1 cup liquid during the cooking process.

- Add liquid only to cover the ingredients when making soup, since the vegetables will add more liquid as they cook; you can always add more liquid after cooking for a thinner soup.

- For creamy soups, stir in milk, evaporated milk, cream cheese, silken tofu, or cream as called for at the end of the cooking time, usually during the last hour.

Beans

- Soaking beans overnight is optional before cooking them in the slow cooker.

- If your recipe includes salt, sugar, or an acidic ingredient such as tomatoes, the beans should be tender before adding them; otherwise, they will stay tough. For more information on cooking beans, see page 180.

Pasta and Rice

- If cooked pasta is to be added to the slow cooker, cook it on the stovetop just until slightly tender before adding it to the crock, to avoid having mushy pasta in your finished dish.

- If a recipe does not call for rice, but you want to add it, use $1/4$ cup extra liquid per $1/4$ cup uncooked rice, and use long-grain converted rice for the best results.

- For long-cooking recipes, stir in cooked rice of any type shortly before serving.

Herbs and Spices

- Quality seasonings make a big difference in the taste of finished recipes, so I recommend you check your spice rack yearly and replace any old herbs and spices.

- Dried herbs and spices can become overpowering and bitter over the long cooking time, so it's best to add them near the end of cooking.

- Fresh herbs tend to disintegrate and taste washed out when added at the beginning of the cooking time, so add them at the end, or use sprigs and discard at the end of cooking.

- Always taste at the end of the cooking time before serving and adjust the seasonings, if necessary.

Oils

- While most slow cooker dishes go right into the crock, others use a bit of oil for browning meats before they're

---

·· The Traveling Slow Cooker ··

Slow cooker meals travel well to picnics, potlucks, family gatherings, and vacation homes. Some slow cooker models feature lock tops and insulated carrying cases, so consider these when deciding which cooker to purchase.

You can wrap a fully cooked meal, within the metal housing and crock, in a towel or layers of newspaper to keep it warm while you transport it. Attach thick rubber bands around the handles of the cooker to keep the lid in place. Be sure to set the cooker on a flat surface so it will not tip over. Upon arrival, serve the food immediately or plug in the cooker and set it to KEEP WARM or LOW.

The temperature of the food you are transporting, as well as the outdoor temperature, will determine how long the food will keep and still be safe to eat. A meal that has just finished cooking, where the crock is too hot to handle without oven mitts, will keep safely for 2 to 4 hours if well wrapped (closer to 2 hours if the outdoor temperature is high and closer to 4 hours if it's cooler outside). Food that has cooled down at all should not be kept longer than 1 to 2 hours before reheating or refrigerating. Meals that have been cooked in the crock and then refrigerated should be wrapped well and reheated or put back in the refrigerator within 2 to 3 hours.

Here's an alternative to wrapping the crock, which I did in my catering days: Place the crock, whether it's just finished cooking or has been cooled and refrigerated, in an insulated cooler. The cooler will keep hot food nice and hot for up to 4 hours and cold food nice and cold for up to 3 hours.

placed in the cooker. Make sure to use good-quality oils. Any oil added to your slow cooker dishes will break down during the long cooking time, so save those beautiful extra-virgin olive oils for adding at the end of the cook time or at serving time. For browning, I use olive or peanut oil. If you use canola oil, only use organic. Sesame oil is used in some recipes for its subtle toasted flavor.

Milk, Cheese, and Other Dairy Products

- Milk, sour cream, and cream break down over long periods of cooking and generally should be added during the last hour.

- Condensed cream soups (including "healthy" or reduced-fat versions) and evaporated milk are good substitutes for milk and can hold up during extended cooking times.

- Cheeses don't generally hold up over extended periods of cooking and tend to separate or curdle when used alone, so they should be added near the end of cooking unless otherwise directed in a recipe.

Convenience Foods

I have never been a proponent of packaged food items. Enter my sister Meg, who scheduled her recipe testing for this book around hustling her husband off to work, chauffeuring her kids where they needed to go, and getting to work herself. "I don't have time to make a homemade barbecue sauce," she said one day. "So I used something out of the pantry as a substitute." As a result, some recipes in this book include convenience foods to make prep times shorter for busy working cooks.

When buying convenience foods, read the labels carefully and avoid products with long lists of artificial ingredients. You don't need a big pantry, but there are some basic ingredients you should have on hand so you can devise meals at the last minute. Following are some that I always try to have in my cupboard:

- Jarred marinara and Alfredo sauces

- Salsa

- Barbecue sauce

- Roasted red and green chiles and enchilada sauce

- Polenta in a tube

- Condensed soups (cream of mushroom, cream of chicken, and condensed chicken broth)

- Canned low-sodium chicken, vegetable, and beef broth

- Canned beans

- Sun-dried tomatoes

- Dry onion soup mix

Hot Drinks and Dips

Hot drinks and dips are fun foods, perfect for birthdays and weekend family dinners. Your large slow cooker can double as a punch bowl for wonderfully imaginative and tasty hot drinks during the cooler months. And it makes a great steaming witches' cauldron at Halloween! Slow cooker hot punches and flavored milks can be made ahead, and the KEEP WARM setting will warm your brew for hours, letting individuals ladle their own cupfuls.

With all hot drinks, be sure to use heat-proof ladles, mugs, or other glassware. Don't use your everyday drinking glasses in case they are not heatproof; they may crack or shatter when filled with hot liquid. For the serving ladle, use one big enough so it won't slip down into the slow cooker between guests' serving themselves. Stay away from metal ladles, as they can chip the earthenware crock.

Dips are often served as a little something for a casual get-together or as a prelude to a meal. Children love to dip, so make a dip the centerpiece of a light meal, with bread and vegetables for dunking.

Dips are easy to throw together and can feed a large group effortlessly.

Do you love fondue but hate to pull out the fondue pot just to make one recipe once in a while? Look no further than your slow cooker. Mix fondue ingredients together right in the ceramic insert, then let the cooker warm the mixture, and serve it hot right out of the crock.

Fondues and dips can sit for hours on the LOW or KEEP WARM setting. Serve them with toasted baguette slices, fresh bread, cut-up pita, raw or blanched vegetables, or a host of chips for dipping.

Buttered Mulled Apple Juice

R emember hot buttered rum? Here is a nonalcoholic version in which un-sweetened apple juice is served with a pat of butter melting into the brew. You can float the spices in the hot juice, wrap them in a cheesecloth bag, or place them in a tea ball. You can also use aromatic mulled spice tea bags, which are sold during the winter holidays; use one bag to 2 to 3 cups of juice. This is the most wonderful drink on a wintry night or after soccer practice on a cold, raw day. If you like, serve it with a cinnamon stick in the cup for stirring or a strip of candied orange peel if you want to look fancy. ○ *Makes about twelve 8-ounce servings*

COOKER: Large round or oval
SETTING AND COOK TIME: LOW for 4 to 6 hours

2 quarts unfiltered apple juice
Juice of 1 orange
Juice of 1 lemon
⅓ cup firmly packed light brown sugar
Three 4-inch cinnamon sticks
1 teaspoon whole cloves
1 teaspoon allspice berries
½ cup (1 stick) cold unsalted butter, cut into 6 slices, then halved on the diagonal
Angostura bitters (optional)

1. Combine the apple and citrus juices in the slow cooker. Add the brown sugar, cinnamon sticks, cloves, and allspice. Cover and cook on LOW for 4 to 6 hours.

2. Remove the whole spices with a mesh ladle strainer; discard. Serve the juice hot, ladled into heatproof mugs with a half pat of butter on top and a splash of Angostura bitters, if using.

Hot Fruit Punch

This is a family favorite, especially for birthday parties. You don't even have to thaw the concentrates. If making this for a party, float some fresh whole strawberries in the punch for a pretty presentation.

○ *Makes about twelve 8-ounce servings*

COOKER: Large round or oval
SETTING AND COOK TIME: LOW for 3 to 5 hours

One 6-ounce can frozen orange or tangerine juice concentrate
One 6-ounce can frozen lemonade concentrate
One 6-ounce can frozen pineapple juice concentrate
10 cups water
Three 4-inch cinnamon sticks
½ teaspoon whole cloves
1 orange, cut into 6 slices, then each cut in half, or 2 Meyer lemons, each cut into 6 slices

1. Combine the concentrates and the water in the slow cooker. Add the cinnamon sticks and cloves. Cover and cook on LOW for 3 to 5 hours.

2. Remove the whole spices with a mesh ladle strainer; discard. Serve the punch hot, ladled into heatproof mugs, with an orange or lemon slice perched on the side of the cup.

·· Party Nuts ··

I always make sure to put out a small bowl of spiced nuts for parties, as they go well with hot drinks. Left over, they taste great in salads. The slow cooker toasts nuts beautifully, with little risk of burning them.

Buttery Rosemary Pecan Halves o Makes 4 cups

Buy the most perfect pecan halves you can find, the bigger the better. These delicious, savory nuts are a surprising treat; addiction is a possibility. Serve warm.

COOKER: Medium round or oval
SETTINGS AND COOK TIMES: HIGH for 15 minutes, then LOW for 1½ to 2 hours

4 cups (1 pound) pecan halves
3 tablespoons unsalted butter, melted
1 tablespoon dried rosemary, crumbled
½ teaspoon cayenne pepper
2 to 3 teaspoons fine sea salt, to your taste

1. Combine the nuts, melted butter, rosemary, and cayenne in the slow cooker. Stir with a wooden spoon to coat the nuts evenly. Cover and cook on HIGH for 15 minutes, then reduce the heat to LOW and cook, uncovered, stirring occasionally, for 1½ to 2 hours.

2. Sprinkle the salt on the nuts and toss to distribute evenly. Transfer to a baking sheet lined with parchment paper or aluminum foil and let cool completely. The nuts will keep, at room temperature in a tightly covered container, for up to 3 days.

Hot Raspberry Cider

I adore anything made with raspberries. Be sure to use a nice unfiltered, unsweetened apple juice—look for a fresh one in the refrigerated section of the supermarket. ○ *Makes about twelve 8-ounce servings*

COOKER: Large round or oval
SETTING AND COOK TIME: LOW for 3 to 5 hours

One 6-ounce can frozen raspberry juice concentrate
2 quarts unfiltered apple juice or fresh apple cider
2 cups water
Three 4-inch cinnamon sticks
1 orange, cut into 6 slices, then each cut in half

1. Combine the raspberry juice concentrate, apple juice, and water in the slow cooker. Add the cinnamon sticks and orange slices. Cover and cook on LOW for 3 to 5 hours.

2. Serve hot, ladled into heatproof mugs.

Fresh Ginger Ale

Oh yes, there is such a thing as homemade ginger ale. First you make and chill the ginger syrup, then add it to seltzer, club soda, or sparkling water for a fabulously refreshing cold drink, perfect for the summer.

Makes about twelve 12-ounce servings

COOKER: Small oval or medium round or oval
SETTING AND COOK TIME: LOW for 5 to 6 hours

About 1½ pounds fresh ginger, peeled and coarsely chopped or thinly sliced
    (by hand or in a food processor) to make 2 full cups
2 cups sugar
Four 2-inch-long strips lemon zest, removed with a vegetable peeler
2 cups water
Ice cubes for serving
Seltzer, club soda, or sparkling water for serving

1. Combine the ginger, sugar, lemon strips, and water in the slow cooker. Cover and cook on LOW for 5 to 6 hours.

2. Let cool to room temperature and pour through a mesh strainer. Pour the strained liquid into a covered container or pitcher and chill. The ginger syrup will keep, refrigerated, for up to 1 week.

3. To serve, place ice cubes in twelve tall 12-ounce glasses, then add ¼ cup of the ginger syrup to each glass. Fill to the top with the seltzer. Taste and add more ginger syrup if you want a stronger flavor. Serve immediately.

Hot Almond Milk with Saffron

I had this drink at an Indian dinner, sipping it for dessert alongside some cookies, instead of coffee or tea. This hot nut milk can be served for breakfast, too. Use only a pinch or two of the saffron; you want a barely discernible whisper of its flavor, not a dominant taste. ○ *Makes about eight 8-ounce servings*

COOKER: Medium round or oval
SETTING AND COOK TIME: LOW for 3 to 5 hours

Two 32-ounce boxes almond milk
2½ tablespoons sugar
Pinch or two of saffron threads
1 tablespoon green cardamom pods, crushed lightly and
     wrapped in a cheesecloth bag
¼ cup slivered blanched almonds

1. Place the almond milk, sugar, and saffron in the slow cooker. Add the spice bag. Cover and cook on LOW for 3 to 5 hours.

2. When ready to serve, remove and discard the spice bag. Use an immersion blender to foam the hot drink. Alternatively, you can ladle the hot milk into a blender and pulse for several seconds to make the foam. Pour the hot almond milk into cups and serve immediately with a few almonds sprinkled over the froth.

Hot Cocoa with Marshmallows

I'm a connoisseur when it comes to unsweetened cocoa powder. I used to use Droste, but then I graduated to Scharffen Berger, which has an incredible, and quite addictive, chocolatey flavor. Valrhona is a close second, with good old Hershey's coming in third. Using a great cocoa powder will really improve the taste of your hot cocoa. The other wonderful touch to perfect hot cocoa is to find house-made marshmallows, which are usually cubed since they are cut by hand instead of extruded; you can sometimes find them in the bakery section of a gourmet supermarket. The condensed milk serves as the sweetener, so you won't need to add any sugar. You can double or triple this recipe for a crowd; if you do so, be sure to use a large slow cooker. ○ *Makes about six 10-ounce servings*

COOKER: Medium round or oval
SETTING AND COOK TIME: LOW for 3 to 5 hours

⅓ cup unsweetened cocoa powder
6 cups milk or soy milk
1 tablespoon pure vanilla extract
One 14-ounce can nonfat sweetened condensed milk
8 to 12 marshmallows

1. Place the cocoa and 2 cups of the milk in the slow cooker; whisk by hand or use an immersion blender to combine until smooth. Add the remaining 4 cups milk, the vanilla, and the condensed milk, stirring to combine. Cover and simmer on LOW for 3 to 5 hours.

2. Briskly stir the cocoa with a whisk before serving. Ladle the steaming cocoa into mugs; top with 1 or 2 marshmallows and serve.

Butter Bean Hummus

Making your own hummus allows you to prepare it just the way you like it, adjusting both the consistency and the spicing to your own taste. Here it is made with butter beans, the flavorful extra-large limas, instead of the traditional chickpeas. Be sure to use an extra-virgin olive oil; you really want to taste it. Serve the hummus as a dip drizzled with olive oil along with pita flatbread, whole-grain crackers, or vegetables (such as romaine lettuce spears, cherry tomatoes, sliced cucumber, and celery stalks) to scoop it up. Or use it as a sandwich spread or a filling for stuffed wraps. ○ *Makes 4 cups*

COOKER: Medium round or oval
SETTING AND COOK TIME: HIGH for 2 to 3 hours, then let
    beans stand in turned-off cooker for 1 hour

1 cup dried large lima beans
5 cups boiling water, or as needed to cover
1 to 2 cloves garlic, to your taste
¼ cup tahini (sesame seed paste)
¼ cup freshly squeezed lemon juice, or more as needed
1½ teaspoons salt, or to taste
Pinch of cayenne pepper
½ to 1 cup extra-virgin olive oil, to your taste

1. Place the lima beans in a colander and rinse under cold running water. Pick them over, discarding any that are discolored. Place them in the slow cooker along with the boiling water to cover by 2 inches. Cover and cook on HIGH for 2 to 3 hours, until the beans are quite tender but still hold their shape and the transparent skin that covers each bean slips off easily. The beans should be covered with liquid at all times. Turn off the slow cooker, uncover, and let the beans stand in the cooker for 1 hour, until warm.

2. Drop the garlic into a food processor and finely chop. Drain the beans, reserving some of the cooking liquid. Add the warm beans to the garlic in the food processor along with the tahini, lemon juice, salt, and cayenne. Pulse until the hummus is quite smooth. Add the olive oil, drizzling it in (some people like lots of olive oil, others less), then add the reserved bean cooking liquid, pulsing after each addition, until the desired consistency is reached. If you are going to use the hummus as a dip, you want a texture similar to that of guacamole. If you are going to use it as a sandwich spread, it should be a bit thicker. Taste the hummus and adjust the seasonings as desired. It will keep, refrigerated, for up to 4 days.

Slow Cooker Tip: Power Outages During Slow-Cooking

If you are not at home during the entire cooking process and the power goes out, throw away the food even if it looks done. If you are at home, finish cooking the ingredients immediately by some other means: on a gas stove, on the outdoor grill, or at a house where the power is on. If the food was completely cooked just as the power went out, it should remain safe up to two hours in the cooker with the power off.

Hot Tofu Artichoke Dip

hildren adore this dip. It is mild and no one will guess the creamy element is the silken tofu. Don't use firm or extra-firm tofu; they will not work.

○ Makes about 3 cups; serves 8

COOKER: Small round or oval
SETTING AND COOK TIME: LOW for 1½ to 2½ hours

2 to 3 cloves garlic, to your taste
One 13.75-ounce can artichoke hearts packed in water, drained
⅓ cup freshly grated Parmesan cheese
4 ounces silken tofu
¾ cup plain thick yogurt (preferably Greek style) or sour cream
¼ teaspoon salt
Pinch of cayenne pepper or chili powder

1. In a food processor fitted with the metal blade, drop the garlic through the feed tube to chop. Add the remaining ingredients and pulse until a smooth puree forms, stopping to scrape down the bowl as necessary. Scrape the dip into the slow cooker. Cover and cook on LOW for 1½ to 2½ hours, until the dip is hot throughout.

2. Set the slow cooker in the serving area. With the cooker set on LOW and the cover off, serve with crackers and pita bread triangles for dipping.

Poker Party Creamy Cheesy Chili Dip

My sister Meg has been making this dip for years; she adapted it to the slow cooker so it would stay warm for a whole poker party. You can halve this recipe and make it in a small oval cooker. ○ *Makes about 3 cups; serves 12*

COOKER: Medium round or oval
SETTING AND COOK TIME: LOW for 2 to 3 hours

Two 14.5-ounce cans meat chili with beans
½ cup sour cream
½ cup shredded sharp cheddar cheese
Two 8-ounce packages cream cheese, cut into pieces
2 bags Fritos Scoops! corn chips

1. Place the chili, sour cream, and cheddar in the slow cooker; stir to combine. Stir in the cream cheese. Don't worry that it is in chunks; it will melt. Cover and cook on LOW for 2 to 3 hours, until the dip is hot throughout and the cheese is melted. Stir the dip once or twice during the cooking time.

2. Set the slow cooker in the serving area. With the cooker set on LOW and the cover off, serve with the corn chips for dipping.

Hot Parmesan, Feta, and Olive Dip
with Herbed Pita Chips

T here is something wonderful about the combination of Parmesan cheese and olives. When the dip is heated, the Parmesan melts and is ever so tasty. The feta gives it some body and adds a bit of a tart flavor. Be sure to rinse the feta before you crumble it to eliminate extra salt. Use whichever kind of olive you like best, from canned California black olives to kalamatas from the deli olive bar. Don't skip the parsley, even though it seems like a lot. I've included a recipe for homemade pita chips, but most supermarkets and gourmet food shops carry a range of commercial pita chips in case you are in a hurry. ● *Makes about 4 cups; serves 12*

COOKER: Small oval
SETTING AND COOK TIME: LOW for 2 to 4 hours

1 cup (4 ounces) freshly grated Parmesan cheese
One 16-ounce container sour cream
4 ounces feta cheese, crumbled
¼ cup finely chopped fresh Italian parsley
¼ cup chopped pitted black olives
¼ cup chopped jarred roasted red peppers or half of a 4-ounce jar pimientos
1 small clove garlic, pressed

HERBED PITA CHIPS:
4 pita rounds
3 tablespoons olive oil or nonstick olive oil spray
⅓ cup freshly grated Parmesan cheese
1½ teaspoons crumbled dried oregano
1½ teaspoons crumbled dried basil
½ teaspoon paprika

1. Place the Parmesan, sour cream, feta, parsley, olives, peppers, and garlic in the slow cooker; stir to combine. Cover and cook on LOW for 2 to 4 hours, until the dip is hot throughout and the cheeses are melted.

2. Meanwhile, preheat the oven to 350°F and make the pita chips. Cut the pitas into triangles and place on a baking sheet. Brush or spray each with olive oil (spraying is the easiest). Combine the Parmesan, oregano, basil, and paprika in a small bowl; lightly sprinkle over the pitas. Bake until just crisped, 5 to 7 minutes. Remove from the oven and set aside to cool.

3. Set the slow cooker in the serving area. With the cooker set on LOW and the cover off, serve with the pita chips for dipping.

Slow-Steamed Artichokes with Red Pepper Aioli

A ioli, which is simply a garlic mayonnaise, is a very popular condiment that can serve as the base for all sorts of flavors, such as the red peppers here. Whenever I see jumbo artichokes in the market, I know it is time to make this recipe. You slow-steam some big artichokes in the cooker, then serve them with the homemade mayonnaise. The oval slow cooker is the best shape for cooking whole artichokes, as it can hold them in one layer. This is a really impressive presentation, with one giant artichoke stuffed in the center with the creamy dip and the other artichokes set around it for dipping. ● *Serves 6*

COOKER: Large oval
SETTING AND COOK TIME: LOW for 6 to 8 hours

4 to 6 large artichokes, plus 1 very large artichoke
1½ cups water
2 tablespoons olive oil
4 lemon slices

RED PEPPER AIOLI:
1 clove garlic
2 tablespoons chopped fresh basil
¼ cup jarred roasted red peppers, drained
1 cup mayonnaise
½ cup sour cream

1. Cut the stem flush with the bottom of each artichoke so they can stand flat. Cut 1 inch off the top and, with kitchen shears, snip the tip off each exposed leaf. Arrange them stem end down, packed together, and standing up in the slow cooker. Add the water and olive oil, then place the lemon slices in the water. Cover and cook on LOW for 6 to 8 hours, until the leaves are very tender and separate with no resistance when pulled off. Remove the artichokes from the cooker with tongs. Let cool to room temperature (if not using right away, cover with plastic wrap and store in the refrigerator for up to 2 days).

2. Meanwhile, make the aioli. In a food processor with the machine running, drop the garlic through the feed tube to chop. Turn the machine off and add the basil, then the red peppers; pulse a few times to chop. Add the mayonnaise and sour cream; pulse to combine. The aioli will keep, in a tightly covered container in the refrigerator, for up to 1 day.

3. Pull open the inner leaves on the very large artichoke and remove them, leaving the outer leaves intact like a shell. Scrape out the inedible prickly choke with a spoon. Fill the large artichoke with the aioli and place it in the center of a serving platter. Cut the rest of the artichokes in half, clean the chokes out of each with a spoon, and arrange the halves around the aioli-filled artichoke. Alternatively, pull off all the leaves and arrange them around the aioli-filled artichoke. Scrape the choke from the artichoke bottoms, cut the bottoms in half, and arrange them with the leaves on the platter for dipping.

Meg's Prosecco Fondue

Prosecco is a sparkling wine created from Prosecco grapes grown in the northern Veneto region of Italy, the foothills of the Alps. It is often substituted for Champagne. Prosecco teams up wonderfully with three cheeses in this delicious fondue you can serve as an appetizer or family meal paired with a green salad. My sister Meg likes to dip big chunks of bread in the fondue, as do her kids. Think of it as kind of a drippy grilled cheese sandwich. Be sure to coat the cheese with the cornstarch; it's key to keeping the hot cheese emulsified, while the lemon juice protects the cheese from getting stringy. Serve with one of the hot juices in this chapter to drink while dipping. ● *Serves 4*

COOKER: Medium round or oval
SETTINGS AND COOK TIMES: HIGH for 30 minutes, then LOW for 1 hour

1 clove garlic, split
1½ cups Prosecco
2 tablespoons freshly squeezed lemon juice
2 cups (8 ounces) shredded Emmenthaler cheese
2 cups (8 ounces) shredded Gruyère cheese
1 cup (4 ounces) cubed fontina cheese
1 tablespoon cornstarch
2 to 3 grinds of black pepper, to your taste
Pinch of paprika
1 to 2 loaves country French bread, cut into 2-inch chunks
2 to 3 apples, cored and sliced

1. Combine the garlic, Prosecco, and lemon juice in the slow cooker, cover, and cook on HIGH for 30 minutes while preparing the cheeses.

2. Combine the cheeses in a large bowl and toss with the cornstarch. When the Prosecco is hot, remove the garlic clove and add the cheese slowly, a handful at a time, letting each addition melt before adding the next and stirring to keep lumps from forming. Reduce the heat to LOW, cover, and cook until the cheese is melted, about 1 hour. The fondue will keep in the slow cooker on LOW for up to an additional hour before serving. The melted cheese will be the consistency of a light cream sauce.

3. Stir the pepper and paprika into the fondue right before serving. With the slow cooker set on LOW and the cover off, serve the fondue with the bread and apple slices for dipping.

·· What to Dip in a Fondue ··

You cannot eat fondue without having something to dip into it. Here are some suggestions:

- **Breads:** Crusty country French or Italian bread, baguettes, white or whole-wheat pita wedges, tortillas, tortilla chips, croissants, bread sticks, naan, chapati, focaccia, or baked polenta cubes.

- **Blanched vegetables:** Broccoli and cauliflower florets, asparagus, green beans, snow peas, or snap peas. Blanch in a pot of lightly salted boiling water for 1 to 2 minutes to soften them up just a bit. Drain well on a double layer of paper towels before putting them out on a serving plate by the fondue.

- **Steam 1 to 2 pounds new potatoes or sweet potatoes in their jackets until knife-tender, about 10 minutes.** Let cool and cut into thick cubes or slices. Arrange on a platter and refrigerate until serving. Serve in place of bread cubes.

- **Raw vegetables:** Cherry tomatoes, baby carrots, jicama, red bell pepper strips, celery sticks, or whole mushrooms.

Cheese and Green Chile Fondue
with Potato Dippers

This fondue is a real winner. Use potatoes as the dipper instead of bread. They taste so good paired with the green chiles. Serve with a salad of leafy greens and fresh tomatoes tossed with olive oil and vinegar. ● *Serves 4 to 6*

COOKER: Medium round or oval
SETTINGS AND COOK TIMES: HIGH for 30 minutes, then LOW for 1 hour

1 clove garlic, split
1¾ cups dry white wine
2 cups (8 ounces) shredded Swiss or Gruyère cheese
2 cups (8 ounces) cubed or shredded Monterey or Teleme Jack cheese
3 tablespoons all-purpose flour
One 4-ounce can diced roasted green chiles, drained
Pinch of cayenne pepper
2 pounds large waxy potatoes or sweet potatoes

1. Rub the inside of the crock with the garlic clove. Pour in the wine and cook on HIGH, uncovered, for 30 minutes to evaporate some of the wine.

2. Toss the cheeses with the flour in a large bowl. When the wine is hot, add the cheese slowly, a handful at a time, letting each addition melt before adding the next and stirring to keep lumps from forming. Add the chiles and cayenne. Set the cooker to LOW, cover, and cook until the cheese is melted, about 1 hour. The fondue will keep in the slow cooker on LOW for an additional hour before serving. The melted cheese will be the consistency of a light cream sauce.

3. Meanwhile, in a medium-size saucepan with a steamer insert, steam the whole potatoes in their jackets until just tender, not mushy, about 10 minutes. Let cool and cut into thick slices. Arrange on a platter and refrigerate until serving.

4. With the slow cooker set on LOW and the cover off, serve the fondue with the potato slices for dipping.

Favorite Family Breakfasts

The slow cooker is well known for its convenience in getting dinner on the table with little muss or fuss, but what about breakfast? The slow cooker comes to the rescue again, delivering delicious egg dishes and breakfast cereals.

Many slow cookers come with a warning advising you not to use the machine to prepare dishes with eggs or dairy products. This is good advice for eight-hour all-day cooking, as eggs and dairy products do not cook well over long periods of time. But if you are cooking these dishes for less than four hours, or if you add the dairy at the very end of cooking, there is no problem. Just be sure not to let your finished egg dish sit for any prolonged amount of time in the crock before serving it—it's best to serve it as soon as it's done.

I use only Grade AA brown or white free-range or cage-free eggs because I think they taste better. There is a marked difference between organic and conventional eggs, since the chickens producing organic eggs dine upon organic, unsprayed vegetarian feed and are not treated with hormones or antibiotics. If you live in an area where someone is selling extra eggs from their own chickens, or if you have your own flock of "girls," you will be as-sured of really fresh eggs for your egg dishes. If you are on a restricted diet and cannot eat eggs, there are many commercial egg substitutes available (powdered, refrigerated, or frozen) that you can use in preparing the recipes in this chapter. These products work fine in the slow cooker.

The slow cooker and hot breakfast cereals were made for each other. Steel-cut oats can be cooked overnight on LOW, so they are ready and waiting for you when you wake in the morning. There are a few other basic grains that are great for break-fast, such as cornmeal, couscous, and mixed-grain cereals. I also like to use a 10-grain cereal mix from Bob's Red Mill (www.bobsredmill.com), which, like steel-cut oats, can be left to cook overnight.

Cheddar-Egg Strata

A strata is a layered egg, milk, bread, and cheese casserole that cooks up like a dense soufflé and is very popular for brunch. Serve this strata with a side of pan-grilled sausages, a ham steak, or crab cakes. ● *Serves 6*

COOKER: Large oval
SETTING AND COOK TIME: LOW for 4 to 5 hours

1 loaf sliced French country or hearty white bread (10 to 12 slices,
    crusts removed if very chewy), torn into pieces
3 cups (12 ounces) shredded sharp cheddar cheese
6 large eggs
1½ cups half-and-half
1½ cups whole milk
¼ teaspoon salt
¼ teaspoon paprika
1 teaspoon Dijon mustard
Splash of Worcestershire sauce

1. Coat the inside of the crock with nonstick cooking spray. Add half of the bread pieces to the crock and sprinkle with half of the cheese. Make another layer of bread and cheese.

2. In a medium-size bowl, whisk together the eggs, half-and-half, milk, salt, paprika, mustard, and Worcestershire sauce; pour over the bread. Press down gently to soak all the bread.

3. Cover and cook on LOW for 4 to 5 hours, until the sides are browned and the center is set. An instant-read thermometer inserted in the center should register 190°F. Let the casserole rest, covered, in the turned-off cooker for 10 minutes before serving.

Crustless Bacon and Broccoli Quiche

Be ready to eat right when this quiche is done cooking for the best texture and flavor. You can use other vegetables here instead of the broccoli, such as artichoke hearts, green beans, or pepper strips, which are all available frozen.

o *Serves 6*

COOKER: Large oval
SETTING AND COOK TIME: LOW for 3½ to 4 hours

8 slices bacon
2 tablespoons unsalted butter, softened
10 large eggs
1 cup half-and-half or evaporated skim milk
A few grinds of black pepper
2 cups (8 ounces) shredded Swiss cheese, such as Jarlsberg or Gruyère
One 10-ounce package frozen chopped broccoli, thawed and pressed to
    remove excess moisture

1. Cook the bacon in a medium-size heavy skillet until crisp. Drain on paper towels, then chop or tear into pieces.

2. Rub the bottom and 1 inch up the side of the crock with the butter. In a medium-size bowl, beat the eggs and half-and-half together. Add the pepper, then stir in the cheese, broccoli, and cooked bacon. Pour the mixture into the slow cooker, cover, and cook on LOW for 3½ to 4 hours. Do not overcook or else the eggs will become too firm.

3. Portion the quiche out of the crock with a plastic spatula and serve immediately with juice, toast, and jam.

Tortilla-Egg Casserole

 Here is a delightful version of eggs, tortillas, and salsa, layered in the slow cooker. Serve with juice and a fruit salad. Olé! ○ *Serves 8*

COOKER: Large round or oval
SETTING AND COOK TIME: LOW for 3 to 4 hours

12 large eggs
1 cup milk
12 flour tortillas, 8 left whole and 4 cut in half
4 cups (1 pound) shredded cheddar cheese
3 cups chunky tomato salsa
One 16-ounce container sour cream, stirred together with the juice and grated
    zest of 2 limes, for serving
1 to 2 ripe avocados, peeled, pitted, and sliced, for serving

1. Coat the inside of the crock with nonstick cooking spray. In a large bowl, whisk the eggs and milk together until a bit foamy; set aside.

2. Lay 1½ tortillas in the crock to cover the bottom. Ladle in ½ cup of the egg mixture, then top with ¾ cup of the cheese and ⅓ cup of the salsa. Repeat the layers of tortillas, egg mixture, cheese, and salsa until all the ingredients are used up, ending with a layer of egg, salsa, and cheese. Additional cheese can be added if you'd like the top of the casserole completely covered with cheese. Cover and cook on LOW for 3 to 4 hours, until the eggs are set and the edges are browned.

3. Serve portions topped with a dollop of the lime sour cream and avocado slices on the side.

Green Chile Slow Cooker Omelet with Warm Fresh Tomato Salsa

R emember oven omelets and frittatas? Well, they're perfect candidates for the slow cooker. When I traveled in Mexico, a small restaurant called Café Gemini became a favorite breakfast haunt. Usually I was the first customer of the day and the owner would be placing cups of warm, freshly cooked salsa on each table. Here I re-create that wonderful salsa, which cooks while the omelet does. Serve the omelet with the warm salsa and a stack of fresh corn tortillas. ○ *Serves 6*

COOKER: Omelet, Large oval; Salsa, Medium round or oval
SETTINGS AND COOK TIMES: Omelet, LOW for 3½ to 4 hours; Salsa, HIGH for 2½ to 3 hours

2 tablespoons unsalted butter, softened
12 large eggs
¼ cup olive oil
⅓ cup all-purpose flour, sifted
A few grinds of black pepper
2 cups (8 ounces) shredded Monterey Jack cheese or Mexican-blend cheese
One 7-ounce can roasted whole green chiles, drained and coarsely chopped

TOMATO SALSA:
12 ripe Roma plum tomatoes, cored and left whole
2 cloves garlic
1 to 2 jalapeño peppers, to your taste, stems cut off and an X cut in the opposite end
2 medium-size white boiling onions, cut in half
¼ cup fresh cilantro leaves
Salt to taste

1. Rub the bottom and 1 inch up the inside of the large crock with the butter. In a large bowl, beat the eggs and oil with a whisk. Sprinkle in the flour and whisk together. Add the pepper, then stir in the cheese and green chiles. Cover and cook on LOW for 3½ to 4 hours, until the eggs are set and the edges are browned. Do not overcook or else the eggs will become too firm.

2. Once you've got the eggs in the crock, immediately prepare the salsa. Coat the inside of the medium-size crock with olive oil nonstick cooking spray. Make a slice in the sides of 2 of the tomatoes and push a clove of garlic inside each. Place all of the tomatoes in the crock. Add the whole jalapeño peppers, or, if you don't like a spicy salsa, cut them in half and scrape out and discard the seeds. Add the onions. Cover and cook on HIGH for 2½ to 3 hours, until all of the vegetables are tender. Add the cilantro. (You can remove the jalapeños if you want a very mild salsa.) Using an immersion blender, puree to a smooth consistency. Season with salt. Serve hot, warm, or at room temperature, or make ahead and chill. The salsa will keep, tightly covered in the refrigerator, for up to 1 week. (You can rewarm the salsa in the microwave or on the stovetop in a small saucepan over low heat.)

3. Divide the omelet into six equal portions, then lift each portion out of the crock with a plastic spatula and serve immediately with the warm salsa.

"Brinner" Cinnamon French Toast Casserole

My sister Meg's sons love breakfast for dinner, which her elder son, Nicolas, calls "brinner." This is essentially an eggy sweet bread pudding. For a complete meal, serve this for brunch or Sunday night dinner with bacon or sausage, and a fruit salad. ○ *Serves 6*

COOKER: Large oval
SETTING AND COOK TIME: HIGH for 2½ to 3 hours

One 1-pound loaf sliced cinnamon swirl bread, each slice cut into quarters
2 tablespoons cold unsalted butter, cut into thin slices
8 large eggs
1½ cups half-and-half
1½ cups whole milk
¼ cup pure maple syrup
¼ teaspoon ground nutmeg
¼ teaspoon salt

TOPPING:
3 tablespoons unsalted butter, cut into small pieces
½ cup firmly packed brown sugar
½ cup old-fashioned rolled oats (not quick-cooking)
½ teaspoon ground cinnamon

1. Coat the inside of the crock with nonstick cooking spray. Add half of the bread quarters to the crock and sprinkle with the slices of butter. Add the remaining bread quarters.

2. In a large bowl, whisk together the eggs, half-and-half, milk, maple syrup, nutmeg, and salt; pour over the bread. Press down gently to soak all the bread.

3. In a small bowl, combine the topping ingredients and use your fingers or two forks to work them together until crumbly. Sprinkle over the top of the bread mixture. Cover and cook on HIGH for 2½ to 3 hours, until the sides are browned and the center is set. An instant-read thermometer inserted in the center should register 190°F.

4. Let the casserole rest, covered, in the turned-off cooker for 15 minutes before serving.

Ham and Sunflower Seed Frittata

I have been making this yummy recipe for ages. It is the brainchild of my friend Lou Pappas, a food writer, cooking teacher, and caterer. The recipe first appeared in her book *Egg Cookery* (101 Productions, 1976), where it was called Hungarian Ham Squares. It is a firm egg casserole, being most tender when it is nice and hot, but it can also be eaten at room temperature. Serve with a salad or sweet rolls. ○ *Serves 4*

COOKER: Medium oval
SETTING AND COOK TIME: LOW for 3 to 4 hours

1 tablespoon unsalted butter, softened
6 large eggs
¾ cup plain yogurt or sour cream
Pinch of salt
A few grinds of black pepper
6 ounces cooked ham, finely chopped to make 1 cup
2 green onions, chopped
2 tablespoons chopped fresh Italian parsley
¼ cup hulled raw sunflower seeds
½ cup shredded Swiss cheese, such as Jarlsberg or Gruyère

1. Rub the bottom and 1 inch up the inside of the crock with the butter. Add the eggs and yogurt to the crock and whisk together. Add the salt and pepper, then stir in the ham, onions, parsley, sunflower seeds, and cheese. Cover and cook on LOW for 3 to 4 hours, until the eggs are set and the edges are browned. Do not overcook or else eggs will become too firm.

2. Portion out of the crock with a plastic spatula and serve immediately.

Overnight Steel-Cut Oats Oatmeal

O ne of the most popular ways to use a slow cooker is to make oatmeal with steel-cut oats, also marketed as Irish or Scottish oats. Everyone I know who has ever prepared overnight oatmeal with steel-cut oats has never gone back to stovetop oatmeal—it's that good. Steel-cut oat nibs, which are whole groats cut into two or three chunks, are notorious for the long soaking and cooking required to soften them properly, so cooking them overnight in the slow cooker works brilliantly. These proportions make a moderately thick porridge; if you like it thicker, cut back the water by $1/2$ to 1 cup the next time you make it. ○ *Serves 2*

COOKER: Small or medium oval
SETTING AND COOK TIME: LOW for 8 to 9 hours

1 cup steel-cut oats
4 cups water

1. Combine the oats and water in the cooker. Cover and cook on LOW for 8 to 9 hours, until tender.

2. Stir well and scoop into serving bowls with an oversize spoon. Serve with milk or cream, and brown sugar or maple syrup.

How to Use the Smart-Pot Slow Cooker Machine

What if you want to make a dish that cooks for six hours but you won't be home for eight hours? Until now, you had no choice but to overcook the food or make something else. Now there is another option. Rival, maker of the Crock-Pot line of slow cookers, created the Smart-Pot, a slow cooker that is easily programmable, even by the legions of us who can't figure out our DVD players.

There are two styles of Smart-Pot. One type can cook on the HIGH setting for 4 or 6 hours, or on the LOW setting for 8 or 10 hours. When the cooking time is up, the Smart-Pot will automatically shift to the KEEP WARM setting (which is recommended for no more than 4 hours), so your meal is waiting for you when you are ready to eat. With this type of Smart-Pot, if you want to cook for a period of time that is different than the automated setting allows (for example, less time on LOW or a longer time on HIGH), you'll have to be there to turn the pot OFF or ON. Please note that even though this is an automatic machine, you *cannot* preprogram the cooking start time, letting uncooked food sit in the crock, and begin cooking at a later time, because the food will spoil rapidly. The Smart-Pot simply allows you to program how long to cook the food.

The second type of Smart-Pot is more flexible. You can set it to cook on HIGH or LOW for anywhere from 30 minutes up to 20 hours, in half-hour increments. Here is how to use it: Fill the crock as usual, then place it into the housing and put on the cover. Plug in the Smart-Pot. The cooker's three lights—marked HIGH, LOW, and KEEP WARM—will all flash, alerting you that it is time to select the setting you wish to use. Push the round button on the left, which is marked HIGH, LOW, and KEEP WARM, top to bottom. One push selects LOW, two pushes select HIGH, and three pushes select KEEP WARM. (If you set the Smart-Pot to KEEP WARM, you cannot set a cooking time. It will stay on KEEP WARM until you manually turn it off.) If you have chosen LOW or HIGH, you will now set the cooking time. Press the button with the up-pointing arrow. The first push puts 30 minutes on the digital display, and every subsequent push adds 30 minutes more. If you accidentally put more time on the cooker than you wanted, don't worry. Just push the button with the down-pointing arrow and watch the display decrease in 30-minute increments. When the cooking time is up, the cooker will automatically switch to the KEEP WARM setting, which will keep the food hot until you are ready to eat it.

This Smart-Pot is also equipped with an OFF button, so you can easily end the cooking earlier than planned. If you wish, you may leave the cooker turned off but plugged in when you are not using it. (I don't recommend this, however. It's too easy for the empty cooker to be turned on accidentally.)

Oatmeal with Cranberries and Apple

Here is another fabulous overnight oatmeal made with steel-cut oats. If you would like a richer flavor, before putting the oats in the crock, toast them on a baking sheet at 350°F for 15 minutes, stirring occasionally. ● *Serves 2*

COOKER: Medium round or oval
SETTING AND COOK TIME: LOW for 7 to 9 hours

1 cup steel-cut oats
½ cup fresh or dried cranberries
1 cup peeled, cored, and chopped apple
¼ cup firmly packed brown sugar
½ teaspoon ground cinnamon
4 cups water

1. Combine the oats, cranberries, apple, brown sugar, cinnamon, and water in the slow cooker. Cover and cook on LOW for 7 to 9 hours, or overnight.

2. Stir well and scoop into serving bowls with an oversize spoon. Serve with milk and maple sugar or syrup.

Slow Cooker Tip: Is the Slow Cooker Safe?

Yes, emphatically yes, the slow cooker is very safe for cooking food. The direct, multidirectional heat from the pot, lengthy cooking time, and concentrated steam created within the tightly covered container combine to destroy bacteria and make the slow cooker a safe process for cooking foods.

Old-Fashioned Oatmeal

O atmeal made overnight in the slow cooker with regular rolled oats is creamy, nourishing, and, most important, ready when you are. No early-morning fumbling for measuring cups is required. The earliest riser in the family can grab a bowlful, then replace the slow cooker lid to keep the rest of the oatmeal warm for the late sleepers. Remember that your oatmeal is only as good as the kind of oats you put in the pot; quick-cooking and instant varieties have no place here. Be sure to use old-fashioned rolled oats. ○ *Serves 4*

COOKER: Small or medium oval
SETTING AND COOK TIME: LOW for 7 to 9 hours, or HIGH for 2 to 3 hours

2 cups old-fashioned or thick-cut rolled oats
4 ¾ cups water
Pinch of salt

1. Combine the oats, water, and salt in the cooker; stir to combine. Cover and cook on LOW for 7 to 9 hours, or overnight, or on HIGH for 2 to 3 hours.

2. Stir well and scoop into serving bowls with an oversize spoon. Serve with milk, buttermilk, or cream, and a sprinkle of toasted wheat germ, brown sugar, and cinnamon.

Irish Oatmeal with Vanilla and Maple

The mellow flavors of vanilla and maple extracts are natural partners with the buttery taste of oats. Real oats lower your blood serum cholesterol, and just a small bowl satisfies your appetite so that you don't have cravings or snack your way to lunch. McCann's Irish Oatmeal from County Kildare, Ireland, is my favorite brand for this morning cereal; you can recognize it by the beautiful white, gold, and black can in which it is packaged. Visit www.mccanns.ie to find out where to purchase it if your supermarket does not carry it. ● *Serves 4*

COOKER: Small or medium oval
SETTING AND COOK TIME: LOW for 7 to 9 hours, or HIGH for 2 to 3 hours

1 cup McCann's Irish steel-cut oatmeal (not the instant or quick-cooking kind)
2 tablespoons toasted wheat germ, plus more for sprinkling
2 tablespoons flax seed (available in health food stores)
1 tablespoon sugar
¼ teaspoon salt
2½ cups water
1 teaspoon pure vanilla extract
¼ teaspoon pure maple extract
½ cup raisins or dried blueberries (optional)

1. Combine the oats, wheat germ, flax seed, sugar, salt, and water in the slow cooker; stir to combine. Cover and cook on LOW for 7 to 9 hours, or overnight, or on HIGH for 2 to 3 hours.

2. Stir in the extracts and raisins, if using, then scoop into serving bowls with an oversize spoon. Serve with milk, buttermilk, or cream, and a sprinkle of wheat germ, brown sugar, and cinnamon.

Breakfast Couscous with Dates and Nuts

ouscous is a form of pasta that is indigenous to northern Africa. It is usually served with savory dishes as a side starch. Here is a sweet version of a recipe called *farka* from Tunisia; every bite is absolutely packed with dates and nuts. It is as easy as oatmeal to prepare and every bit as satisfying. ○ *Serves 4*

COOKER: Medium round or oval
SETTING AND COOK TIME: LOW for 6 to 7 hours

1⅓ cups regular or whole-wheat couscous (about 1 pound)
½ cup sugar
Pinch of fine sea salt
2 cups water
3 tablespoons unsalted butter
½ cup chopped nuts, such as pistachios or almonds, toasted in a 350°F oven until
    lightly golden, 4 to 5 minutes
1 cup chopped pitted dates (4 ounces)

1. Combine the couscous, sugar, salt, and water in the slow cooker. Add the butter, nuts, and dates; stir. Cover and cook on LOW for 6 to 7 hours, or overnight; the cereal will be thick.

2. Stir well and scoop the cereal into serving bowls with an oversize spoon. Serve with hot milk or soy milk and honey or brown sugar.

Slow Cooker Main-Dish Salads and Sandwiches

Salads and sandwiches out of the slow cooker? Who would have thought?

Main-dish salads are a practical summer meal. And the salads in this chapter are not simple wedges of lettuce served on the side but substantial salads capable of carrying the whole meal with style. Prepared with a selection of tasty proteins—meat, poultry, fish, beans—in combination with raw and cooked vegetables, pasta, and a nourishing and appealing

array of greens, these salads will give you plenty to choose from. All you need is some good-quality bread or a basket of muffins, and dinner is on the table.

The sandwiches included in this chapter are perfect for a luncheon buffet, with your guests ladling out the delicious filling straight from the slow cooker. Or change things up and serve sandwiches for dinner—with this kind of hearty, finger-licking fare, no one will go away from the table hungry or disappointed.

Slow Cooker Tip: Keep Your Lid On

Unless a recipe tells you otherwise, do your best to resist your own curiosity and don't lift the lid while your slow cooker is at work. As the contents of the slow cooker heat up and create steam, a natural water seal forms around the rim of the lid and creates a vacuum. The rim of the lid will stick in place when gently pulled. This is important for the even cooking of the food within. But what if a recipe calls for adding ingredients halfway through or near the end of the cooking time, or you want to check your food for doneness? It is fine to lift the lid in these instances, but always remember that by breaking the water seal and allowing the steam to escape, the temperature within is reduced. When you place the lid back on, it takes 20 to 30 minutes for the contents to come back to the proper cooking temperature. You can easily check the contents visually through the glass lid. There is no need to stir or turn the food, unless a recipe specifies to do so. Usually stirring right before serving will suffice.

Turkey Taco Salad

T aco salad, a sort of Mexican chef's salad, is not only fun, it's nutritious. Turkey is a favorite in Mexican cuisine, and the naturally low-fat tenderloin poaches beautifully in the slow cooker. If you cook the beans from scratch, you might want to do that the day before; otherwise, have two slow cookers going during the day, so you will be ready to make the salad in a flash. Order some ultra-tasty heirloom beans from Rancho Gordo (www.ranchogordo.com) for a nourishing and delightful culinary treat.

Makes about 3 cups beans and about 4 cups poached turkey meat, to serve 4

COOKER: Medium or large round or oval
SETTINGS AND COOK TIMES: Beans, HIGH for 3 to 4½ hours; Turkey, HIGH for 2½ to 3 hours

BEANS:
1 cup dried pinto, scarlet runner, anasazi, or borlotti beans
1 dried whole red chile (New Mexican, California, or ancho)
1 small white onion, chopped or cut into wedges
1½ teaspoons fine sea salt, or to taste

TURKEY:
1¼ to 1½ pounds turkey tenderloins (about 2)
Salt and freshly ground black pepper to taste
¼ bunch fresh cilantro, separated into leaves and stems
4 green onions, each cut into 4 pieces
4 lemon slices
Hot water to cover

SALAD:
8 corn tortillas, each cut into 4 wedges
Fine sea salt
6 cups shredded romaine lettuce, tossed with the cilantro leaves (see above)
3 cups diced ripe tomatoes or tomato wedges
3 cups (12 ounces) shredded Monterey Jack cheese

CHIPOTLE CREAM DRESSING:

1 cup mayonnaise

½ cup plain yogurt

1 to 2 canned chipotle chiles in adobo sauce, to your taste, mashed, plus
    2 teaspoons adobo sauce

Juice of 1 lime

GARNISHES:

2 ripe avocados, peeled, pitted, and sliced

⅓ cup chopped green onions

⅓ cup chopped pitted black olives

2 limes, each cut into 6 wedges

1. Place the beans in a colander and rinse under cold running water; pick over for small stones. Place in the slow cooker (there must be plenty of room for them to bubble without spilling over) and cover with cold water; allow to soak for 6 to 12 hours.

2. Drain the beans. Add the chile, the onion, and enough fresh water to cover the beans (4 to 5 cups). Cover and cook on HIGH 3 to 4½ hours. Toward the end of cooking, add the salt and remove and discard the chile. The beans should be covered with liquid at all times to cook properly. When done, the beans should be tender but still hold their shape and not fall apart.

3. Let the beans stand in the cooker for 1 hour, uncovered, then transfer them with their liquor to a covered storage container and refrigerate (they can be made ahead and refrigerated for up to several days or frozen for up to 1 month).

4. Coat the inside of the crock with nonstick cooking spray. Arrange the tenderloins in a single layer in the bottom of the crock. Sprinkle with salt and pepper. Add the cilantro stems, green onions, lemon slices, and enough hot water to barely cover the turkey. Cover and cook on HIGH for 2½ to 3 hours, until the turkey is white throughout when cut with a knife. An instant-read thermometer inserted in the thickest part should register 170°F. Let stand in the hot broth, uncovered, for 15 minutes.

5. Remove the turkey from the broth to a plate or cutting board. If not using immediately, transfer the turkey and liquid to a covered container and refrigerate for up to 2 days. When ready to proceed, shred the turkey with two forks or cut into cubes. (If not using within 2 days, cool and portion the meat into small plastic zipper-top freezer bags and freeze for up to 2 months, then thaw before assembling salad.)

6. Preheat the oven to 400°F. Arrange the tortillas on a large baking sheet, coat both sides with olive oil nonstick cooking spray, and sprinkle with a little salt. Bake until golden, about 10 minutes. Immediately, while warm, arrange the tortillas in the bottom and up the sides of 4 shallow salad bowls. Divide the lettuce and cilantro, turkey, beans, tomatoes, and cheese evenly between the bowls, layering the ingredients in the order given.

7. In a small bowl, stir together the mayonnaise, yogurt, chipotle, adobo, and lime juice. Spoon 3 to 4 tablespoons of the dressing over each salad, top with avocado slices, green onions, and olives, and serve immediately with the lime wedges.

Family-Style Salmon Pasta Salad

One way to serve salmon to a large number of people without breaking the bank, yet still have plenty for a satisfying main dish, is to make a steamed fresh salmon, pasta, and vegetable salad. The oval-shaped slow cooker works best for shallow steam poaching, and the naturally high fat content of the salmon means it is forgiving if it's slightly overcooked. Be sure to pour the boiling liquid around the fish, not over the top. And always use dried pasta for big-bowl salads, since it holds its shape better than fresh pasta. ● *Serves 12*

COOKER: Medium or large oval
SETTING AND COOK TIME: HIGH for 1½ hours

1 lemon, thinly sliced
1 large shallot, minced
1 carrot, quartered
4 sprigs fresh Italian parsley
One 1½- to 2-pound skinned thick center-cut salmon fillet, rinsed, patted dry,
    and any pin bones removed
Salt and freshly ground black or white pepper to taste
½ cup water
½ cup dry white wine or low-sodium chicken broth
2 cups shelled fresh peas or frozen petite peas, thawed
One 1-pound package baby carrots, each cut into 3 pieces
2 pounds medium-size pasta shells
1 pound asparagus, woody stems snapped off, cut into 3-inch lengths

SALAD DRESSING:
1 cup olive oil
⅓ cup champagne vinegar or white wine vinegar
Juice of 2 lemons
2 tablespoons Dijon mustard
2 cloves garlic, pressed

One 12-ounce can large California black olives, drained and quartered
Leaves from 1 bunch fresh Italian parsley or watercress, chopped

1. Coat the inside of the crock with nonstick cooking spray and arrange the lemon slices over the bottom. Sprinkle with the shallot, then lay the carrot pieces and parsley sprigs on top. Arrange the salmon fillet over it all and tuck the ends of the fillet under to even out the thickness of the fish so it cooks evenly. Season the fish lightly with salt and pepper. Heat the water and wine in a small saucepan on the stovetop or in the microwave until boiling. Pour the hot liquid around (not on top of) the salmon. Cover and cook on HIGH for 1½ hours.

2. Carefully lift the fish out of the crock with a large plastic spatula or pancake turner and transfer to a bowl to cool. Use at room temperature or cover and refrigerate overnight. Remove the skin and flake the salmon. Refrigerate until ready to make the salad.

3. Bring a large pot of water to a boil over high heat. When the water comes to a boil, add the peas and carrots, then the pasta. Cook the pasta according to the package directions until it is *al dente*, a bit chewy when bitten into; do not overcook. Add the asparagus during the last 2 to 3 minutes of cooking. Drain the pasta and vegetables in a colander and rinse under cold running water. Let cool to room temperature.

4. In a small bowl, whisk together the olive oil, vinegar, lemon juice, mustard, and garlic. Set aside.

5. Place the pasta mixture in a large, deep salad bowl and toss with the olives, chopped parsley, and flaked salmon. Toss with the dressing until well coated. Cover and refrigerate until ready to serve or overnight. The salad absorbs the dressing as it sits, so you may want to reserve some of the dressing to toss with the salad again right before serving. Serve chilled. Leftovers will keep, tightly covered in the refrigerator, for up to 2 days.

Thai Beef and Pasta Salad

I n this recipe, flank steak is slow-cooked in a nice marinade, then sliced and served on top of a pile of dressed pasta and the fresh-tasting combination of mint, green onion, and cilantro. Top that with roasted peanuts and be ready for a fabulous taste treat. This is one of my favorite creations. ● *Serves 6*

COOKER: Large round or oval
SETTING AND COOK TIME: LOW for 5 to 6 hours

1 large white onion, thinly sliced and separated into rings
One 1½-pound flank steak, trimmed of excess fat and patted dry
4 cloves garlic, minced
¼ cup sugar
¼ cup low-sodium soy sauce
3 tablespoons freshly squeezed lime juice
2 tablespoons peeled and minced fresh ginger
1 tablespoon toasted sesame oil
6 grinds of black pepper

Two 9-ounce packages fresh linguine
¼ cup rice wine vinegar
4 teaspoons low-sodium soy sauce
1 teaspoon ginger juice (from grated and squeezed fresh ginger)
1 teaspoon toasted sesame oil
4 teaspoons Thai sweet chili sauce
½ teaspoon cayenne pepper
Juice of 2 limes
14 fresh mint leaves, finely chopped
1 bunch green onions, chopped
¼ cup finely chopped fresh cilantro
1 bunch watercress, stemmed
¼ cup chopped roasted salted peanuts

1. Coat the inside of the crock with nonstick cooking spray and arrange the onion slices over the bottom. Make very shallow horizontal slits against the grain across the top of the steak, then lay it on top of the onion.

2. In a small bowl, combine the garlic, sugar, soy sauce, lime juice, ginger, sesame oil, and pepper. Pour the mixture over the steak, making sure to coat all exposed surfaces well. Cover and cook on LOW for 5 to 6 hours, checking at 4½ hours, until tender when cut with a knife.

3. Meanwhile, bring a large pot of water to a boil for the pasta. When the water comes to a boil, cut the linguine into 6-inch lengths, add to the water, and cook until *al dente*, 3 to 4 minutes. Drain in a colander and rinse under cold running water.

4. Place the vinegar, soy sauce, ginger juice, sesame oil, chili sauce, cayenne, and lime juice in a jar with a lid; shake vigorously to combine. Place the pasta in a shallow bowl and toss with the mint, green onions, and cilantro. Toss with the dressing. You can let the pasta sit at room temperature or refrigerate it until the meat is done.

5. Remove the meat to a cutting board, cover with aluminum foil, and let it stand for 10 minutes before slicing. On a platter or individual salad plates, make a bed of the watercress and pile the noodles on top. Cut the steak across the grain into ½-inch-thick slices and lay over the noodles. Sprinkle with the peanuts and serve.

Ratatouille and Polenta
on a Bed of Greens

Ratatouille, a regional specialty from Provence, is a juicy mixed-vegetable stew that truly tastes better the day after you make it—served up hot, at room temperature, or cold. Here it is presented as a great main dish salad served with broiled polenta on a bed of leafy greens. Round out the meal with some fresh baguettes and a bowl of piney green extra-virgin olive oil for dipping.   **o** *Serves 4*

COOKER: Medium or large round or oval
SETTING AND COOK TIME: HIGH for 2½ to 3 hours, or LOW for 4 to 5½ hours

4 Japanese eggplants, cut lengthwise into thick slices, then in half across
1 medium-size to large bell pepper (green, red, orange, or yellow), seeded and
    cut into big pieces
2 medium-size yellow onions, coarsely diced
2 cloves garlic, or to taste, minced
One 14.5-ounce can fire-roasted tomatoes, drained
¼ cup olive oil
Sea salt and freshly ground black pepper to taste
2 sprigs fresh thyme
1 small sprig fresh rosemary or basil
1 sprig fresh marjoram
2 medium-size zucchini, cut into thick rounds

BALSAMIC VINAIGRETTE:
¼ cup extra-virgin olive oil
1 tablespoon balsamic vinegar
1½ teaspoons sherry vinegar
½ teaspoon Dijon mustard
1 very small shallot, chopped
Sea salt and freshly ground black pepper to taste

TO SERVE:

One 16-ounce roll polenta, plain or with sun-dried tomatoes

Olive oil as needed

10 to 12 ounces leafy baby greens mix, or a combination of baby greens and
   torn butter lettuce

2 ounces soft goat cheese, crumbled, or ½ cup freshly grated Parmesan cheese (optional)

1. Combine the eggplant, bell pepper, onions, garlic, and tomatoes in the slow cooker. Pour over the olive oil and toss to coat. Season lightly with salt and pepper and arrange the herb sprigs on top. Cover and cook on HIGH for 2½ to 3 hours or LOW for 4 to 5½ hours. Halfway through the cooking time, stir in the zucchini and cover. When done, the vegetables will be cooked but still hold their shape and there will be vegetable liquid. Remove the herb sprigs and discard. Set aside to cool. Proceed with the recipe, or transfer to an airtight container and refrigerate overnight.

2. When ready to serve, make the vinaigrette. In a small bowl with a whisk or an immersion blender, combine the olive oil, vinegars, Dijon, and shallot; whisk for 30 seconds, until smooth and emulsified. Season with salt and pepper.

3. Cut the roll of polenta into eight ¾-inch-thick slices and place on a broiler pan. Brush with olive oil. Broil until sizzling and slightly browned on one side.

4. Arrange the greens on 4 dinner plates. Drizzle each with about 1 tablespoon of the vinaigrette; you want this very lightly dressed. Arrange 2 warm polenta slices on each plate, overlapping in the center. Top with the ratatouille—it can be warm, cold, or room temperature—then sprinkle with the cheese, if using. Serve immediately.

•• Crock-Poached Chicken Breasts ••

Slow-cooking makes the moistest chicken breasts for salads and sandwiches. You can keep a bag of boneless breasts in the freezer, ready to cook at a moment's notice.

 ◉ Makes about 4 cups cubed or shredded poached chicken meat

COOKER: Medium or large round or oval
SETTING AND COOK TIME: HIGH for 2½ to 3 hours

6 boneless, skinless chicken breast halves (about 2 pounds), rinsed in cold water
1½ cups low-sodium chicken broth or water

1. Place the chicken in the slow cooker and pour over the broth; it should just cover the chicken. Cover and cook on HIGH for 2½ to 3 hours, until the chicken is white throughout when cut with a knife. Let stand in the hot broth, uncovered, for 15 minutes if using immediately. Otherwise, let cool completely in the broth, then transfer to a covered container and refrigerate in the broth for up to 2 days.

2. To use, remove the chicken from the broth to a plate. When cool enough to handle, chop or shred as needed, or freeze the breasts whole in heavy-duty zipper-top plastic freezer bags for up to 1 month. If broth was used to cook the chicken, strain the broth through a fine-mesh sieve and reserve for another use

Barbecue Chicken Salad

Homemade barbecue sauce graces this cold salad as a dressing as naturally as it serves as a glaze for crock-roasted chicken and ribs. The flavor is pure comfort. The salad is terrifically easy to whip up once the chicken is poached. If you are not serving the salad immediately, add the corn chips right before serving so they stay crisp. ○ *Serves 6*

1 recipe Crock-Poached Chicken Breasts (opposite), chopped (about 4 cups)

¼ cup minced red onion

2 medium-size red bell peppers, seeded and diced

One 11-ounce can whole-kernel corn, drained, or cooked fresh corn cut from about 3 ears

3 ounces corn chips (about 1½ cups)

3 tablespoons chopped fresh cilantro

BARBECUE DRESSING:

⅔ cup ketchup

3 tablespoons cider vinegar

2 tablespoons olive oil

2 tablespoons Dijon mustard

1 tablespoon Worcestershire sauce

1 tablespoon brown sugar

1 teaspoon chili powder

1 clove garlic, pressed

A few drops of hot pepper sauce, such as Tabasco

Salt and freshly ground black pepper to taste

1. In a large bowl, combine the chicken, onion, peppers, corn, corn chips, and cilantro and mix well.

2. In a small bowl, combine the dressing ingredients; stir with a whisk to mix well. Add the dressing to the chicken mixture and toss to coat evenly. Season with salt and pepper. Serve warm, or cover and refrigerate until chilled before serving.

Curried Chicken Salad with Raisins and Apples in Pitas

This is one of the most delicious versions among the family of chicken salads. If you prefer, serve the chicken salad on a bed of lettuce and eat the warm pita on the side. This is a great way to introduce children to curry, as it is mild and sweet with the raisins and apples. ☉ *Serves 4*

1 recipe Crock-Poached Chicken Breasts (page 58), cubed (about 4 cups),
    chilled or at room temperature
⅔ cup raisins, soaked in hot water for 15 minutes, drained, and patted dry
3 stalks celery, finely chopped
2 medium-size apples, cored and diced
2 green onions, minced
Salt to taste

CURRY DRESSING:
¾ to 1 cup mayonnaise
2 tablespoons mango chutney, store-bought or homemade (page 100)
1 tablespoon curry powder (or more if you like a strong curry flavor)
Juice of 1 lime or 1 Meyer lemon

TO SERVE:
2 whole-wheat pitas, cut in half
Several leaves of lettuce

1. Place the chicken, plumped raisins, celery, apples, and green onions in a large bowl. Sprinkle with a bit of salt. Combine ¾ cup of the mayonnaise with the chutney, curry powder, and lime juice; combine with the chicken mixture and mix well. Add more mayonnaise if needed to achieve your desired consistency.

2. Warm the pitas in a microwave or toaster. Fill each pita half with a lettuce leaf and one-quarter of the chicken salad until packed full and even a bit overflowing. Serve immediately.

French Dip Sandwiches with Crock-Sautéed Green Peppers

Let the slow cooker do all the work to make these fabulous braised beef sandwiches with delicious *au jus* for drizzling the meat and dipping the rolls. The preferred cut here is one of the favorites of the slow cooker, beef rump roast. The rump is a boneless roast that comes from the round, or leg. It is lean, so it takes naturally to being cooked very slowly in lots of liquid to keep it nice and juicy. Pile the meat high on very fresh French bread or hoagie rolls, along with bell peppers you've slow-sautéed in a second slow cooker. ● *Serves 12*

COOKER: Rump roast, Large round or oval; Peppers, Small or medium oval
SETTINGS AND COOK TIMES: Rump roast, LOW for 7 to 9 hours; Peppers, LOW for 4 hours

2 tablespoons olive oil
One 4- to 5-pound beef rump roast
Garlic powder
2 medium-size onions, sliced
One 1-ounce package dry onion soup mix
2 teaspoons sugar
1 teaspoon crumbled dried thyme
½ teaspoon crumbled dried oregano
Two 10-ounce cans condensed beef broth
One 12-ounce bottle light beer

CROCK-SAUTÉED GREEN PEPPERS:
4 large green bell peppers
2 tablespoons olive oil
4 cloves garlic

TO SERVE:
12 French long rolls, split and toasted if desired
12 slices provolone cheese (optional)
Salt and freshly ground black pepper to taste

1. Make the rump roast. Heat the olive oil in a large pot on the stovetop over medium-high heat. Sprinkle the roast with plenty of garlic powder and place it in the pot; brown each side well.

2. Place the sliced onions in the bottom of the slow cooker. Lay the rump roast on top of the onions. Sprinkle with the onion soup mix, sugar, thyme, and oregano, then pour the broth and beer over all. Cover and cook on LOW for 7 to 9 hours, until very tender.

3. While the meat is cooking, make the green peppers in a separate slow cooker. Cut each pepper lengthwise along the creases, remove the stem, seeds, and pithy core, then peel with a swivel-blade vegetable peeler if you like. Cut the peppers into strips slightly less than 1 inch wide. Pour 1 tablespoon of the olive oil in the bottom of the slow cooker. Lay the pepper slices in the cooker, pushing the cloves of garlic into the pile of peppers. Drizzle with the remaining 1 tablespoon olive oil. Cover and cook on LOW for 4 hours, until the peppers are wilted and considerably diminished in bulk. Set aside to cool, and discard the garlic cloves or crush them and use for another dish. You can make the peppers ahead and store them in their accumulated oil in a covered container in the refrigerator for up to 3 days.

4. Remove the roast from the cooker and place it on a cutting board. Cover with aluminum foil and let stand for 15 minutes. Skim any fat from the liquid in the cooker, if necessary. Carve the meat into thick slices and return it to the cooker; set to KEEP WARM and let sit for up to 1 hour so the meat can absorb some of juice.

5. Make the sandwiches: Remove the meat from the crock, dip the cut sides of one roll into the hot liquid, and pile some meat onto the roll. Place some of the sautéed green peppers on top of the meat, season with salt and pepper, then crown with the top half of the roll. Continue with the remaining rolls, meat, and peppers and serve immediately, while the meat is still warm. Serve extra *au jus* for drizzling if you like lots of juice. If you make the rump roast the day before, reheat the thick slices in the braising liquid on the stovetop or in the microwave. If you are putting the cheese on your sandwiches, place one slice on top of the meat and peppers on each sandwich and microwave on High power for 30 seconds to melt the cheese.

Corned Beef Reuben Sandwiches for a Crowd

The corned beef in this recipe is a variation on the molasses and bourbon–glazed corned beef in the first Not Your Mother's cookbook. This version features a luscious apricot-mustard glaze, which has to be one of the all-time best glazes for meat. When you're shopping for sauerkraut, look for the refrigerated brands in a jar or plastic bag—they're usually tastier than canned sauerkraut. You can buy Russian dressing, but the flavor is much nicer if you take a couple of minutes to stir up this quick homemade version yourself. Reubens are usually grilled or broiled, but when serving a crowd, you can skip that step and the sandwiches don't suffer a bit. Be sure to use the freshest rye bread you can find and a top-quality Gruyère cheese. ○ *Serves 12*

COOKER: Large round or oval
SETTING AND COOK TIME: LOW for 9 to 11 hours, then bake corned beef
in 375°F oven for 15 minutes to set glaze

One 4- to 5-pound corned beef brisket with seasoning packet, rinsed
8 black peppercorns
2 allspice berries
1 onion, quartered
4 cloves garlic

APRICOT-MUSTARD GLAZE:
½ cup apricot jam
⅓ cup firmly packed dark brown sugar
⅓ cup Dijon or coarse-grained mustard

RUSSIAN DRESSING:
1 cup mayonnaise
1 tablespoon prepared horseradish
1 teaspoon Worcestershire sauce
¼ cup bottled chili sauce
1 tablespoon grated onion

TO SERVE:

24 slices light rye bread with caraway seeds

12 to 24 slices Gruyère cheese (cut to fit the bread slices)

About 3 cups sauerkraut, or to taste, rinsed in a colander and drained well

1. Lay the corned beef in the slow cooker. If the meat is too big to lay flat, cut it in half and stack the pieces one atop the other. Add water to just cover the brisket. Add the seasoning packet, peppercorns, allspice, onion, and garlic. Cover and cook on LOW for 9 to 11 hours.

2. Meanwhile, mix together the glaze ingredients in a small bowl until smooth; cover and refrigerate until needed.

3. Mix together the dressing ingredients in a medium-size bowl until smooth; cover and refrigerate until needed.

4. When the brisket is fork-tender, preheat the oven to 375°F. Line a large rimmed baking sheet with aluminum foil and coat with olive oil nonstick cooking spray. Lift the brisket out of its cooking liquid and transfer to the baking sheet. Spoon the glaze over the beef to coat the entire surface on all sides. Bake, basting with any remaining glaze, for 15 minutes to set the glaze. Carve into thin slices.

5. To make the sandwiches, spread one side of half the bread slices with a thin layer of dressing, top with 1 to 2 slices of cheese, then a layer of corned beef and a little pile of sauerkraut; top with the remaining bread slices. Serve immediately, while the meat is still warm.

Lynn's Flank Steak Tostadas with Cilantro Yogurt Sauce

Everyone loves tostadas! Here is a recipe using slow-cooked beef, shredded and tossed with a variety of vegetables and piled onto corn tortillas, created by my slow cooker compadre and cookbook author, Lynn Alley. Store any leftover shredded beef in the refrigerator for up to 3 days or portion it into zipper-top plastic freezer bags and freeze for up to 2 months. The cilantro yogurt sauce is luscious and addictive. ● *Serves 4*

COOKER: Large round or oval
SETTING AND COOK TIME: LOW for 8 to 9 hours

3 pounds flank steak, trimmed of all fat
1 teaspoon salt
1 large white onion, cut into large chunks
4 cloves garlic

CILANTRO YOGURT SAUCE:
1 cup (8 ounces) thick plain yogurt (preferably Greek style) or sour cream
Juice of 1 small lime
1 clove garlic, pressed
½ teaspoon salt
1 cup finely chopped fresh cilantro

TO SERVE:
Eight 6-inch corn tortillas
2 medium-size ripe tomatoes, diced
1 cup shredded carrots
1 to 2 ripe avocados, peeled, pitted, and diced
½ cup chopped white onion or green onions
½ green or yellow bell pepper, seeded and minced
3 cups shredded napa cabbage or iceberg or romaine lettuce
½ cup fresh cilantro leaves, for garnish

1. Place the flank steak, salt, onion, and garlic in the slow cooker. Add water just to cover. Cover and cook on LOW for 8 to 9 hours. Remove the meat from the crock and place in a shallow bowl. Let stand at room temperature to cool to warm, then shred it using your fingers (the traditional method) or a fork. If not using immediately, cover and refrigerate for up to 3 days.

2. Prepare the cilantro yogurt sauce. In a food processor or blender, combine the yogurt, lime juice, garlic, salt, and chopped cilantro; pulse until just combined (don't completely puree; bits of the cilantro leaves should remain visible). Transfer to a serving bowl; refrigerate until chilled.

3. Preheat the oven to 450°F. Coat a large baking sheet with nonstick cooking spray. Place the tortillas in a single layer on the sheet and bake until they are crisp and the edges have browned, 5 to 7 minutes.

4. To build the tostadas, place 2 warm tortillas on each plate. Layer each tortilla with some shredded meat, 2 tablespoons each of tomatoes, carrots, and diced avocado, and 1 tablespoon each of onion and bell pepper. Top each tostada with ¼ to ⅓ cup of the cabbage, then a dollop of the yogurt sauce. Garnish with whole cilantro leaves and serve immediately.

Smoky Hand-Pulled Pork on a Bun
with Cabbage-Carrot Slaw

Slow cooker cooking has made pulled pork wildly popular all over America, not just in the South, where it is a beloved local specialty. Be sure to get the meat cooking first thing in the morning if you plan to serve it in the evening. I based this recipe on one from a slow cooker cook-off competition that came with the following recommendation: "This is a great dish for weekends in the country, Friday night dinners, or evenings when you have a house full of teenagers who cannot get enough of the rich, smoky sauce." Enough said. ❍ *Serves 6 to 8*

COOKER: Large round or oval
SETTING AND COOK TIME: LOW for 9 to 10 hours, or HIGH for 5 to 5½ hours

2 tablespoons olive oil
2 medium-size white onions, finely chopped
4 cloves garlic, minced
1 tablespoon chili powder
1 teaspoon freshly ground black pepper
1 cup bottled chili sauce
¼ cup firmly packed light brown sugar
¼ cup cider vinegar
1 tablespoon Worcestershire sauce
½ to 1 teaspoon liquid smoke, to your taste
One 3-pound boneless pork shoulder, trimmed of excess fat

CABBAGE-CARROT SLAW:
6 cups finely shredded green cabbage (about two-thirds of a 2-pound cabbage)
1 cup shredded carrots
½ cup thin green bell pepper strips
1 cup mayonnaise
2 tablespoons cider vinegar
2 tablespoons light brown sugar
Salt to taste

8 fresh kaiser rolls, onion buns, or other soft sandwich rolls,
    split in half and warmed

1. In a medium-size skillet, heat the olive oil over medium heat. Add the onions and cook, stirring a few times, until softened, about 5 minutes. Add the garlic, chili powder, and pepper and cook for 1 minute. Add the chili sauce, brown sugar, vinegar, Worcestershire sauce, and liquid smoke; bring to a boil.

2. Coat the inside of the crock with nonstick cooking spray. Place the pork in the crock and pour the sauce over. Cover and cook on LOW for 9 to 10 hours or on HIGH for 5 to 5½ hours, until the pork is falling-apart tender.

3. While the meat is cooking, make the slaw. In a large bowl, combine the cabbage, carrots, and bell pepper strips. In a small bowl, stir together the mayonnaise, vinegar, and brown sugar until smooth; add to the vegetable mixture and toss to lightly coat. Season with salt, cover, and refrigerate until ready to serve (this is best enjoyed the day it is made).

4. Transfer the meat to a cutting board and pull the meat apart into shreds using two forks. Return the meat to the crock; you can let it sit on the KEEP WARM setting for up to 2 hours. When ready to serve, place the two sections of a warm bun on a plate, spoon some of the shredded pork and plenty of sauce onto one of the bun halves, top with the remaining bun half, and place some slaw on the side.

Meg's Shredded Barbecue Chicken Sandwiches with Sour Cream Potato Salad and Dill Cucumber Spears

My sister Meg's mother-in-law has been making her famous barbecue sauce for years. It is a tradition for her to light up the charcoal barbecue on her porch all year long in Anchorage, Alaska, except when the temperature is in the negative numbers. Meg adapted the recipe for the slow cooker so that during the week she can enjoy that same barbecue flavor as soon as the family gets home. The sauce is very mild and kid-friendly; when making it for adults who like some heat, just add a bit more red pepper flakes. ● *Serves 8*

COOKER: Large round or oval
SETTING AND COOK TIME: LOW for 5 to 7 hours

DILL CUCUMBER SPEARS:
2 large cucumbers, cut lengthwise into spears
¼ cup seasoned rice vinegar
1 tablespoon dill weed

BARBECUE SAUCE:
2 tablespoons unsalted butter
1 medium-size yellow onion, diced
2 tablespoons Worcestershire sauce
¼ cup freshly squeezed lemon juice
1½ teaspoons dry mustard
⅛ teaspoon red pepper flakes
1½ cups ketchup
1 tablespoon cider vinegar
6 tablespoons firmly packed brown sugar
1 teaspoon salt

CHICKEN:
1½ pounds boneless, skinless chicken breasts
1½ pounds boneless, skinless chicken thighs

SOUR CREAM POTATO SALAD:

2 pounds new white potatoes, quartered, then cut into ¾-inch chunks

¾ cup reduced-fat sour cream

¼ cup light mayonnaise

Salt and freshly ground black or white pepper to taste

½ cup thinly sliced green onions

TO SERVE:

8 soft sesame-seed sandwich rolls

1. Make the cucumber spears. Place the cucumbers in a long container with a cover. Pour the vinegar over the cucumbers and sprinkle with the dill. Cover and refrigerate for at least 6 hours, or up to 3 days.

2. Make the barbecue sauce. In a medium-size saucepan, melt the butter over medium heat until sizzling, then add the onion and cook until softened, about 5 minutes. Add the Worcestershire sauce, lemon juice, mustard, red pepper flakes, ketchup, vinegar, brown sugar, and salt; stir well to combine.

3. Coat the inside of the crock with nonstick cooking spray. Place the chicken in the crock and pour the barbecue sauce over. Cover and cook on LOW for 4 to 6 hours, until the chicken is cooked through and no longer pink inside.

4. Using two forks, shred the chicken right in the crock, then stir the mixture to thoroughly combine the sauce and chicken. Cover and continue to cook on LOW for another hour.

5. While the chicken is cooking, make the potato salad. In a large pot, cover the potatoes with salted cold water. Bring to a boil, then reduce the heat to medium-low and simmer until the potatoes are tender when pierced with the tip of a sharp paring knife, 12 to 15 minutes. Drain well. In a medium-size serving bowl, stir together the sour cream and mayonnaise; add the warm potatoes and gently fold to combine. Season with salt and pepper, then fold in the green onions. Cover and refrigerate for at least 1 hour, or up to 1 day.

6. Serve the chicken spooned onto the sandwich rolls with a side of cold potato salad and a cucumber spear or two.

Mini Turkey Meatball Sliders

Anyone who loves meatballs loves meatball sandwiches, and these sliders (the name for these miniature sandwiches) are irresistible. You can make this sandwich using your choice of a baguette or a small roll, but whatever you choose, it must be very fresh or else it will be too chewy. The secret to being able to eat your slider without the meatballs slipping out is to dig out a bit of the soft inside bread to make a little trench for the meatballs to sit in. I like a bit of butter on my slider, but that is optional. ○ *Makes 10 sandwiches, to serve 5*

COOKER: Large round or oval
SETTINGS AND COOK TIMES: HIGH for about 30 minutes, then LOW for 6 to 8 hours

One 28-ounce jar marinara sauce
One 15-ounce can crushed tomatoes
One 15-ounce can tomato puree
3 tablespoons olive oil
1½ pounds ground dark turkey
1½ cups seasoned dry bread crumbs
¼ cup freshly grated Parmesan or Romano cheese
6 tablespoons minced fresh Italian parsley
2 cloves garlic, pressed
1 large egg, beaten
½ teaspoon salt
A few grinds of black pepper

TO SERVE:
2 fresh 20-inch-long thin baguettes or 10 small hoagie rolls
2 tablespoons butter, softened (optional)
1 bunch arugula, stemmed
5 slices provolone, smoked mozzarella, or Monterey Jack cheese, cut in half

1. Coat the inside of the crock with olive oil nonstick cooking spray. Add the marinara, crushed tomatoes, tomato puree, and olive oil. Stir to blend, cover, and cook on HIGH while you prepare the meatballs.

2. Place the ground turkey in a medium-size bowl, breaking it up a bit with your fingers or a large fork. Add the bread crumbs, Parmesan, parsley, garlic, egg, salt, and pepper. Mix well using your hands or a large fork. Be careful not to compact the meat, which will make your meatballs tough. If the mixture is very soft, cover and place it in the freezer for 20 minutes for easier handling. Divide the meat mixture in half. On a cutting board, lightly pat one half into a thick rectangle. With a table knife, divide the rectangle into 4 equal portions. Roll 5 meatballs from each portion, for a total of 20 meatballs, each about 2 inches in diameter. Repeat with the remaining portion of meat, to make 40 meatballs total.

3. Gently add the meatballs to the crock and spoon some sauce over them. Cover and reset the heat to LOW. Cook for 6 to 8 hours, until the meatballs are firm and an instant-read thermometer inserted into the center of one registers 160°F. If making ahead, let the meatballs cool in the sauce and refrigerate, tightly covered, for up to 3 days, or freeze for up to 2 months.

4. To make the sliders, slice the baguettes into 4-inch sections. Make a horizontal cut to slice each section in half, but don't cut all the way through. Remove and discard a small bit of bread from the tops and bottoms to create a cradle for the meatballs. Spread the baguettes with a bit of soft butter if you like. Place a few arugula leaves on the bottom of each baguette. Set 4 meatballs on each roll and spoon some sauce on top. Top each sandwich with a piece of cheese and press down the tops of the rolls. Serve warm with plenty of napkins.

Sloppy Janes

S loppy Joes are a perennial American favorite. Here is its kid sister, the sloppy Jane, made with ground turkey in place of the beef. Be sure to use dark turkey meat, not white, which will cook up much too dry and tough. Traditionally, these sandwiches are eaten on soft buns, but I like them piled into whole-wheat pitas. If you double this recipe, make sure to use a large slow cooker. ❍ *Serves 4*

COOKER: Medium or large round or oval
SETTING AND COOK TIME: LOW for 6 to 7 hours, or HIGH for 3 to 4 hours

2 pounds ground dark turkey
1 large onion, finely chopped
½ large bell pepper (red, green, yellow, or orange), seeded and finely chopped
2 stalks celery, finely chopped
1 clove garlic, minced
One 8-ounce can tomato sauce
½ cup ketchup
3 tablespoons tomato paste
2 tablespoons cider vinegar
2 tablespoons brown sugar
1 teaspoon chili powder
½ teaspoon paprika
1 tablespoon Worcestershire sauce
Dash of Tabasco sauce
Salt to taste
Soft whole-wheat hamburger buns or other soft sandwich rolls

1. Coat a large nonstick skillet with nonstick cooking spray and set over medium heat. Add the turkey, onion, bell pepper, celery, and garlic, and cook, stirring frequently to break up the meat.

2. When the meat is cooked through, transfer the mixture to the slow cooker. Add the tomato sauce, ketchup, tomato paste, vinegar, brown sugar, chili powder, paprika, Worcestershire sauce, and Tabasco; stir to combine. Cover and cook on LOW for 6 to 7 hours or on HIGH for 3 to 4 hours.

3. Taste for salt and add more vinegar or sugar if desired. Serve the meat mixture spooned onto the split hamburger buns, along with a knife and fork.

Barbecue Tofu Sandwiches

Just in case you need to make a special barbecue-flavored sandwich for the vegetarians in your life, here is a recipe in which tofu is slow-cooked in a zesty homemade barbecue sauce. Tofu is notoriously bland on its own, but it makes a great canvas for assertive sauces. You need to use extra-firm tofu so it will hold its shape in the slow cooker. I like these sandwiches topped with caramelized onions, but they are just as good plain. You can also served the barbecue tofu as a salad piled on a bed of lettuce. ○ *Serves 8*

COOKER: Medium round or oval
SETTING AND COOK TIME: LOW for 4 to 6 hours

Three 16-ounce blocks extra-firm tofu, drained
2 cups ketchup
¼ cup firmly packed brown sugar
3 tablespoons low-sodium soy sauce
2 tablespoons cider vinegar
1 tablespoon Dijon mustard
1 teaspoon paprika or smoked paprika
½ teaspoon garlic powder
¼ teaspoon lemon pepper seasoning
¼ teaspoon Angostura bitters (optional)

TO SERVE:
8 long hoagie rolls, split in half and warmed
Butter lettuce or arugula leaves
Crock-Caramelized Onions (optional; opposite page)

1. Cut each block of tofu into four ³⁄₄-inch-thick slabs and place in a single layer on a baking sheet lined with a triple layer of paper towels. Blot the tops with a paper towel and leave the paper towel there, then place a second clean baking sheet on top and weight it down with unopened canned goods. Let stand for 15 minutes to 1 hour to press out extra liquid from the tofu.

2. In a medium-size bowl, combine the ketchup, brown sugar, soy sauce, vinegar, mustard, paprika, garlic powder, lemon pepper, and Angostura bitters, if using; stir to combine.

3. Coat the inside of the crock with nonstick cooking spray. Cut the tofu into cubes, place them in the crock, and pour the sauce over the tofu. Cover and cook on LOW for 4 to 6 hours, until very hot and fragrant.

4. To make the sandwiches, place a split hoagie roll on a plate. Pile some lettuce on one side and spoon some tofu and sauce on top. Top with caramelized onions, if using. Serve with a knife and fork.

•• Crock-Caramelized Onions ••

Caramelized onions are a condiment that can be made ahead and kept in the refrigerator, just waiting for a hot or cold sandwich that needs that little something extra on top. They are also great in stews. Long cooking transforms the sharp taste of onion into a sweet and savory delight. Be sure to check the onions at 6 hours since some slow cookers run at higher temperatures than others and the onions could burn. To ensure safety and control over the cooking process, never leave the house with your cooker set on HIGH. ● Makes about 3 cups

COOKER: Medium round or oval
SETTING AND COOK TIME: HIGH for 6 to 8 hours

3 to 3½ pounds extra-large sweet yellow onions (2 to 4 onions)
One 10.5-ounce can condensed chicken or beef broth
¼ cup (½ stick) unsalted butter, cut into pieces

1. Coat the inside of the crock with nonstick cooking spray. Cut the onions in half, and cut each half into ½-inch-thick half-moons by hand, with a mandoline, or in a food processor. Place the onions in the crock and add the broth and butter. Cover and cook on HIGH for 6 to 8 hours, until golden brown and very soft.

2. Uncover and let cool completely. Store the onions in their liquid in an airtight covered container in the refrigerator for up to 2 weeks or in the freezer for up to 2 months.

Soup, Beautiful Soup

Old-fashioned soups defy the can-opener culture—they are simple and easy as can be to make in the slow cooker. Take advantage of farmers' markets and make soups that complement the seasons and please your palate. Use the freshest ingredients and quality canned goods for the best-tasting soups. Into the crock go juicy chickens, meat, sausage, onions, herbs, rice, beans, and/or pasta. A few hours later, you have a soup ready to please an army of diners or your family of four, or to pack in a thermos for lunch on the go.

This collection of soups is different from those in my other slow cooker cookbooks: It was assembled with pleasing a family in mind. From creamy tomato-basil to split pea with bacon to vegetable, bean, and pureed soups made with carrots and winter squash, these are designed to satisfy kids and grownups alike.

Tips for the Best Slow Cooker Soups

- Soups cook best if all the ingredients are cut to a uniform size so that they cook evenly. Take the time needed for their proper preparation.

- If you like, you can sweat some of the vegetables, such as onions and garlic, in butter or oil on the stovetop before adding them to the crock. This is a nice flavor addition, although optional.

- Add enough water or broth to at least cover the solid ingredients in the slow cooker. Add boiling liquid to adjust the consistency of the soup at any time during the cooking. Any vegetables in the soup will also add liquid as they cook.

- Think about how much you wish to serve. If your soup is meant to be a first course, figure about 1 cup of soup per serving. For a family-style main dish, figure 2 cups or more per serving.

- Unless noted otherwise, the LOW setting works best for soups, especially in the new slow cookers where the HIGH setting can produce an intense boil. LOW gives a slow simmer. Why rush?

- Use herbs and spices sparingly and always taste for the seasonings at the end of cooking. Slow cookers tend to intensify flavorings. Fresh herbs are best added at the end of cooking.

- As simple and easy as it is to prepare soups in the slow cooker, it is important not to overcook them to the point that the vegetables become a murky mess with little flavor. Pay attention to the times recommended in the recipes.

- To puree a soup, you can use a hand-held immersion blender (one of my favorite kitchen tools), taking care not to hit the sides of the crock, or transfer the soup in batches to a food processor and pulse until smooth. Some soups are best put through a coarse metal sieve if they contain vegetables with tough fibers, like artichokes or asparagus.

•• Croutons for Soups ••

Any good day-old bread, from a baguette to pumpernickel or whole wheat, can be turned into great soup croutons. Basic soup croutons, essentially dried bread cubes, are tossed into soups, while larger croutons are either placed in the bottom of the bowl or floated in the soup.

Oven Soup Croutons: Preheat the oven to 375°F. If the bread is soft, cut it into ¾-inch-thick slices, then cut the slices into thick cubes. If the bread is dense, like rye bread, cut it into thinner slices and smaller cubes. Place on an ungreased baking sheet, drizzle the bread cubes with melted butter or olive oil, and bake until crisp and dry, stirring about every 5 minutes to keep them from burning. Remove from the oven when just golden and drizzle with more melted butter or olive oil. Leave plain or sprinkle with a few tablespoons of grated Parmesan. (To make flavored croutons, sprinkle the hot croutons with 2 tablespoons minced fresh or dried herbs or spices, such as dill or paprika, and some grated Parmesan cheese as soon as they come out of the oven.) Croutons are best used the day they are made.

Italian Sausage Soup
with Spinach Fettuccine

E ver since I discovered how delicious sweet Italian sausages are, I have been on a mission to find new recipes using them. Here is a scrumptious soup, needing only salad and bread to make a satisfying meal, adapted from a favorite soup in *The Loaves and Fishes Cookbook* (Macmillan, 1985). Remember that the sausages must be fully cooked before adding them to the other ingredients in the crock. ● *Serves 6*

COOKER: Large round or oval
SETTING AND COOK TIME: LOW for 5 to 7 hours

1½ pounds sweet Italian sausage, casings removed
1 medium-size yellow onion, chopped
Two 14.5-ounce cans diced tomatoes with their juice
Four 14.5-ounce cans low-sodium chicken broth
¼ cup dry red wine, such as Merlot
½ teaspoon crumbled dried basil
½ teaspoon crumbled dried marjoram
3 medium-size zucchini, halved lengthwise and thinly sliced into half-moons
1 large bell pepper (red, green, yellow, or orange), seeded and diced
One 16-ounce package fresh spinach fettuccine
Salt and freshly ground black pepper to taste
Freshly grated Parmesan cheese for serving

1. In a large skillet over medium-high heat, cook the sausage until browned, breaking it up into smaller pieces. Remove it from the pan with a slotted spoon and drain on paper towels. Drain the fat from the pan, reserving 2 tablespoons. Add the onion and cook, stirring, until softened, about 5 minutes.

2. Place the tomatoes, broth, wine, herbs, zucchini, and bell pepper in the slow cooker. Add the sausage and onion. Cover and cook on LOW for 5 to 7 hours.

3. Bring a large pot of lightly salted water to a boil. Add the pasta and cook according to the package directions until *al dente*, on the chewy side. Drain well and add the cooked pasta to the slow cooker. Cover and let stand for 10 minutes. Season with salt and pepper.

4. Serve in wide soup bowls with plenty of grated cheese for sprinkling on top.

Vegetable, Beef, and Barley Soup with Whole-Grain Beer Bread

I would be remiss if I didn't include this soup, which is a favorite. Years ago, I visited food writer Marion Cunningham, author of the 100th anniversary edition of *The Fannie Farmer Cookbook* (Knopf, 1996), to have her critique my fledgling bread experiments. She served a rich, homemade, brothy beef soup for lunch, and it was memorable. It is important to brown the meat before putting it in the slow cooker, to get the rich color and flavor. If you have some Better Than Bouillon organic soup base in the fridge, in beef, mushroom, or vegetable flavor, add a tablespoon of it to the soup, if you like. This soup conveniently cooks all day, so it is ready for supper. This pairs well with the homemade beer bread, but is just as good served with lots of crackers. o *Serves 8*

COOKER: Large round or oval
SETTING AND COOK TIME: LOW for 7 to 8 hours

3 tablespoons light olive oil
1½ pounds boneless lean beef for stew, cut into ½- to 1-inch cubes
Salt and freshly ground black pepper to taste
Garlic powder to taste
1 medium-size yellow onion, diced
Three 10.5-ounce cans condensed beef broth
6 cups water
4 stalks celery, chopped
4 carrots, cut into 1-inch cubes
2 medium-size new potatoes, cut into 1-inch cubes
½ cup chopped fresh Italian parsley
1 cup pearl barley
1 teaspoon crumbled dried thyme

WHOLE-GRAIN BEER BREAD:

1 cup whole-wheat or white whole-wheat flour

1 cup all-purpose flour

½ cup rolled oats, regular or quick-cooking (not instant)

2 tablespoons light brown sugar

2 tablespoons ground flax meal (available in health food stores)

2 teaspoons baking powder

½ teaspoon baking soda

½ teaspoon salt

1½ cups light beer, just opened (not flat), cold or at room temperature

1. In a large skillet over medium-high heat, heat the olive oil, then brown the beef cubes on all sides, about 5 minutes. Season with salt, pepper, and garlic powder.

2. Coat the inside of the crock with nonstick cooking spray. Remove the browned meat from the skillet with a slotted spoon and place in the crock. Cook the onion in the hot skillet until softened, about 5 minutes, stirring a few times. Pour 1 can of the broth into the skillet and bring to a boil, scraping up the browned bits on the bottom of the pan; pour into the crock. Add the rest of the broth and the water to the crock, then the vegetables, parsley, barley, and thyme. Cover and cook on LOW for 7 to 8 hours, until the beef and barley are tender to the bite.

3. While the soup is cooking, make the beer bread. Preheat the oven to 400°F. In a large bowl with a dough whisk or in the work bowl of a stand mixer with the flat paddle attachment, combine the flours, oats, brown sugar, flax meal, baking powder, baking soda, and salt. Add the beer and stir until just combined. Scrape into a greased 4 x 8-inch loaf pan and bake until the top is dry and a tester inserted into the center comes out clean, 35 to 40 minutes. Let cool for 10 minutes, then remove from the pan.

4. Ladle the hot soup into deep bowls, and serve with thick slices of fresh beer bread and butter. Beer bread is best served the day it is made, but it also tastes great when toasted a day or two later.

Not Your Mother's Chicken Noodle Soup

N o other soup typifies soul-satisfying home cooking like chicken noodle soup. It is the soup that makes you happy, the soup that makes you feel better, the soup that says, "I love you." Homemade chicken stock is not only a delight, but also an essential ingredient in soup making. Many cooks are wary of making their own stock, but this version, which is nice and chicken-y, is really one of the easiest, especially in the slow cooker; you just toss everything in, turn it on, and let it simmer away. The best stocks are never boiled, just simmered slowly, and the slow cooker is excellent at this. In place of the carrot and parsnip, you can also use whole baby carrots with green tops (if you can find them): Trim the roots and leave a dash of green, and add them whole to the soup; they look delightful floating with the fat noodles. Just as my grandmother did, I use the wide dried egg noodles that are found in the section of the supermarket that has Jewish foods, but you can also use fideos (an angel hair pasta bunched to look like a little nest), frozen thick noodles, or medium-size dried egg noodles. ● *Serves 8*

COOKER: Large round or oval
SETTINGS AND COOK TIMES: Stock, HIGH for 1 hour, then LOW for 4 to 5 hours;
   Soup, LOW for about 6 hours

STOCK:
4 cups low-sodium chicken broth
8 cups water
6 chicken bouillon cubes or 2 tablespoons concentrated chicken bouillon
   (I use Better Than Bouillon organic chicken base)
1 yellow onion, quartered
2 stalks celery with leaves, chopped
4 sprigs fresh Italian parsley with stems
Three ½-inch-thick slices peeled fresh ginger
A few grinds of black pepper or a few black peppercorns
2 whole bone-in chicken breasts, split, with skin left on

6 tablespoons (¾ stick) unsalted butter

1 medium-size onion, finely chopped

3 stalks celery, chopped

1 medium-size carrot, diced

1 medium-size parsnip, peeled and diced

2 teaspoons minced fresh marjoram or 1 teaspoon crumbled dried marjoram

2 teaspoons minced fresh thyme or 1 teaspoon crumbled dried thyme

¼ cup minced fresh Italian parsley

Salt and freshly ground black pepper to taste

4 to 8 ounces dried egg noodles

1. Make the chicken stock. Place the chicken broth, water, bouillon, onion, celery, parsley, ginger, pepper, and chicken breasts in the slow cooker. Cover and cook on HIGH for 1 hour, then LOW for 4 to 5 hours; the chicken should be fully cooked and white throughout when cut with a knife. Uncover and let cool for 20 minutes if making the soup immediately. Otherwise, let sit until warm, remove the breasts, and strain the stock as directed in step 2, place the chicken breasts back into the broth, then transfer to a covered container and refrigerate in the stock for up to 2 days.

2. To make the soup, remove the chicken breasts from the stock to a plate. When cool enough to handle, chop or shred; you will have 5 to 6 cups meat. Discard the skin and bones. Set a large colander lined with cheesecloth or a fine-mesh sieve over a large bowl and pour the stock through to strain. Press on the vegetables to extract all the liquid and discard the vegetables. Wash the crock.

3. Place the strained stock in the clean crock, cover, and set on HIGH if using cold broth or LOW if it is still warm.

4. In a small skillet over medium heat, warm the butter until sizzling, then cook the onion and celery, stirring a few times, until softened, about 5 minutes; add to the crock along with the carrot and parsnip. Cover and cook on LOW for about 5½ hours, until the vegetables are tender. Add the cooked chicken and the herbs, and season with salt and pepper. Cover and cook for another 30 minutes.

5. Add the noodles, cover, and cook for 10 minutes, until the noodles are tender. Serve hot in large soup bowls.

After Thanksgiving
Turkey Rice Soup

T here is no soup that tastes quite like turkey soup. And the secret is in the stock. Take your Thanksgiving turkey carcass and turn it into a nice rich stock. Pull off the meat after dinner and get the stock going right away, before the frame dries out. You will have to break up the carcass by separating the ribs from the backbone; it won't fit whole into the pot. Make this vegetable and rice soup with your delicious golden stock. ● *Serves 8*

COOKER: Large round or oval
SETTINGS AND COOK TIMES: Stock, HIGH for 2 hours, then LOW for 8 to 10 hours;
    Soup, HIGH for 1 hour, then LOW for 6 to 8 hours

STOCK:
1 roasted turkey carcass with some meat left on, broken up, including the wings and skin
1 large yellow onion, quartered
1 large leek (white part only), halved lengthwise, washed well, and cut into chunks
4 stalks celery with leaves, plus the heart, cut into chunks
6 sprigs fresh parsley or cilantro, with stems
1 teaspoon crumbled dried thyme or 2 sprigs fresh thyme
2 teaspoons black peppercorns
Concentrated chicken bouillon (I use Better Than Bouillon organic chicken base)
Salt to taste

1 large onion, finely chopped
2 stalks celery, finely chopped
2 medium-size carrots, finely chopped
6 ounces white mushrooms, quartered
1 cup frozen baby lima beans, thawed
One 14.5-ounce can diced tomatoes, drained
⅓ cup chopped fresh Italian parsley
⅓ cup raw converted rice or wild rice
4 cups cooked leftover turkey meat (about 1 pound), cut into bite-size pieces
Salt and freshly ground black pepper to taste

1. Place the broken-up turkey carcass, vegetables, herbs, and peppercorns in the slow cooker. Add water 1 cup at a time until water covers everything by about 4 inches, but do not fill the cooker more than three-quarters full to allow for bubbling up. Add 1 teaspoon bouillon for every cup of water. Cover and cook on HIGH for 2 hours, until hot. Skim off any surface foam with a large spoon. Reduce the heat to LOW and simmer for 8 to 10 hours. If the water cooks down below the level of the ingredients, add more boiling water.

2. Uncover and let cool to lukewarm. Set a large colander or strainer lined with a double layer of cheesecloth over a large bowl and pour the stock through to strain. Press on the vegetables to extract all the liquid. Discard the vegetables, bones, skin, and meat. Season with salt, if desired, or leave unsalted. Refrigerate overnight.

3. After chilling the stock, skim any congealed fat from the surface of the stock. If not using right away, divide the stock into airtight plastic freezer storage containers, leaving 2 inches at the top to allow for expansion in the freezer. The stock can be refrigerated for up to 2 days or frozen for up to 4 months. Makes about 3 quarts.

4. To make the soup, place the stock in the slow cooker, set it to HIGH, and cook until the stock is heated through, about 1 hour. Add the onions, carrots, celery, mushrooms, lima beans, tomatoes, parsley, and rice. Cover and cook on LOW for 6 to 8 hours.

5. Add the turkey meat and cook for 20 minutes. Season with salt and pepper, and serve.

Split Pea Soup with Bacon

Green split pea soup is a perennial favorite. It becomes very thick when chilled in the refrigerator, but, as it is reheated, it will slowly melt. If it is too thick, thin with a bit of water or broth. This soup, which freezes well, is the perfect partner for a grilled cheese sandwich. ● *Serves 6*

COOKER: Large round or oval
SETTING AND COOK TIME: LOW for 8 to 10 hours

One 1-pound bag (2½ cups) dried green split peas
4 ounces thick-sliced smoked bacon, cut into 1-inch-wide strips
1 large yellow onion, diced
2 large carrots, diced
1 medium-size turnip, peeled and diced
1 large russet potato, peeled and diced
2 stalks celery, diced
1 bay leaf
7 cups cold water
A few dashes of hot pepper sauce, such as Tabasco
1½ teaspoons Dijon mustard
Salt and freshly ground black pepper to taste

1. Place the split peas in a colander and rinse under cold running water. Pick them over, discarding any that are discolored. Place the peas in the slow cooker and add hot water to cover. Let stand 1 hour, then drain.

2. In a medium-size skillet over medium-high heat, cook the bacon and onion, stirring, until the onion is softened and the bacon is cooked but not crisp.

3. Place the carrots, turnip, potato, celery, onion-and-bacon mixture, bay leaf, and cold water in the cooker with the peas. Cover and cook on LOW for 8 to 10 hours, until the peas are completely tender. Skim off any scum that rises to the top.

4. Discard the bay leaf. Transfer about half of the soup to a large bowl and puree using an immersion blender, or puree in batches in a food processor or blender. Return the pureed portion of soup to the crock. Stir in the hot sauce and mustard and season with salt and pepper. Ladle the hot soup into bowls and serve immediately.

Vegetable Lentil Soup with Cumin, Coriander, and Lemon

Lentil soup comes in many guises, from complex to simple, but is always at its best with lots of vegetables. This is a great way to stretch your food dollars, as it is a very satisfying, nutritious main-dish soup. You get starch, protein, and vegetables in bite after tasty bite. The spice blend in this recipe was inspired by a soup from a cooking class I attended taught by Edward Espe Brown, author of *Tassajara Cooking* (Shambhala, 1974). ● **Serves 6**

COOKER: Large round or oval
SETTING AND COOK TIME: LOW for 8 to 9 hours

1 medium-size yellow onion, finely chopped
2 stalks celery, finely chopped
2 medium-size new potatoes (red, white, or Yukon Gold), diced
1 medium-size carrot, finely chopped
One 14.5-ounce can diced tomatoes with their juice
1¼ cups dried brown lentils, picked over and rinsed
1 teaspoon ground cumin
1 teaspoon ground coriander
8 cups water
4 vegetable bouillon cubes (I use Rapunzel brand)
Salt and freshly ground black pepper to taste
¼ cup packed chopped fresh cilantro
2 tablespoons freshly squeezed lemon juice
Coarsely grated zest of 1 lemon

1. Coat the inside of the crock with olive oil nonstick cooking spray or rub with olive oil. Place the onion, celery, potatoes, carrot, tomatoes and their juice, lentils, cumin, and coriander in the crock. Add the water and bouillon cubes. Cover and cook on LOW for 8 to 9 hours, until the lentils and vegetables are tender.

2. Season with salt and pepper, then add the cilantro, lemon juice, and lemon zest. Thin with boiling water if the soup is too thick. Ladle into serving bowls and serve hot.

Tuscan Bean Soup

This is a very traditional Mediterranean-style country soup that is made from Spain and Italy to Greece and Turkey. It is adapted for the slow cooker from a recipe in the Nichols Garden Nursery Herbs and Rare Seeds catalog from more than a decade ago. Great Northern beans are the preferred bean in soup making, as they consistently cook up sweet and tender. If you have a Parmesan cheese rind in the fridge, toss that into the soup; it helps make the broth rich. If you like fried sage leaves, simply cook them until crisp in olive oil or butter and add them as a beautiful and flavorful garnish. ○ *Serves 8*

COOKER: Medium or large round or oval
SETTING AND COOK TIME: LOW for 10 hours

One 1-pound bag (2½ cups) dried Great Northern, flageolet, or Romano beans, picked over, rinsed, soaked overnight in water to cover, and drained
1 large yellow onion, finely chopped
2 stalks celery, diced
1 small bulb fennel, fronds removed, bulb cut in half crosswise and thinly sliced
1 large carrot, diced
3 cloves garlic, minced or pressed
¼ cup olive oil
Bouquet garni consisting of 1 sprig fresh oregano or rosemary, 1 sprig fresh sage, 2 sprigs fresh Italian parsley, and 1 small bay leaf wrapped in cheesecloth and tied with kitchen twine
7 cups water
3 tablespoons concentrated chicken bouillon (I use Better Than Bouillon organic chicken base) or 4 to 5 vegetable bouillon cubes (I use Rapunzel brand)
Salt and freshly ground black or white pepper to taste

TO SERVE:
Thin slivers of sliced prosciutto
Freshly grated or shaved Parmesan cheese

1. Place the beans, onion, celery, fennel, carrot, garlic, olive oil, *bouquet garni*, water, and bouillon in the slow cooker. Cover and cook on LOW for 10 hours.

2. When the soup is finished cooking, remove the *bouquet garni* and discard. Transfer one-third of the soup to a large bowl and puree using an immersion blender, or puree in batches in a food processor or blender. Return the pureed portion of soup to the crock. Season with salt and pepper.

3. Ladle the soup into serving bowls and serve hot, topped with slivers of prosciutto and some Parmesan.

Slow Cooker Tip: Slow Cooker Timers

Delay timers are available to use with the slow cooker to help you further preschedule your cook times. For example, you might be making a stew that cooks for 8 hours, but you won't be home for 10 hours. With a delay timer, you can load your ingredients into the crock up to 2 hours before you want the cooker to start cooking. When using a delay timer, make sure that all the ingredients are all well chilled, and never use delay timers with recipes that contain poultry of any type or fish. You can also buy timers that have an extra option to switch the machine to the KEEP WARM setting at the end of cooking.

Black Bean and Rice Soup with Salsa Cream

Here is a hearty vegetarian black bean soup. Black beans are quite easy to digest and exceptionally flavorful, making the once-regional bean a mainstay in the slow cooker kitchen. The fluffy, piquant topping melts delightfully into the soup. Serve with corn muffins. ● *Serves 6*

COOKER: Large round or oval
SETTING AND COOK TIME: HIGH for 2 hours, then LOW for 6 to 8 hours

One 1-pound bag (2½ cups) dried black beans, picked over, rinsed, soaked overnight
    in cold water to cover, and drained
1 large yellow onion, finely chopped
2 cloves garlic, finely chopped
¾ cup raw converted rice
1 teaspoon chili powder
Two 14.5-ounce cans stewed tomatoes with their juice
Two 14.5-ounce cans light vegetable broth or low-sodium chicken broth
Sea salt and freshly ground black pepper to taste

SALSA CREAM:
1 cup cold heavy cream
¼ cup cold sour cream
½ cup chunky tomato salsa
2 tablespoons finely chopped fresh cilantro
Pinch of salt

TO SERVE:
3 limes or lemons, cut into thick wedges

1. Coat the inside of the crock with olive oil nonstick cooking spray. Combine the beans, onion, garlic, rice, chili powder, tomatoes, and broth in the crock. Add water just to cover the beans. Cover and cook on HIGH for 2 hours, then set the cooker to LOW and cook for 6 to 8 hours.

2. Transfer one-third of the soup to a large bowl and puree using an immersion blender, or puree in batches in a food processor or blender. Return the pureed portion of soup to the crock. Season with sea salt and pepper.

3. Meanwhile, make the salsa cream. Whip the heavy cream in a medium-size bowl with a handheld electric mixer on medium-high speed until it forms very soft peaks. Add the sour cream and beat on low speed just to incorporate. Fold in the salsa, cilantro, and salt. Cover and chill for up to 4 hours if not serving immediately.

4. Ladle the soup into serving bowls and serve hot with a spoonful of the salsa cream in the center, which will melt into the soup. Squeeze in lots of lime or lemon juice and serve immediately.

Minestra di Vegetali with White Beans

T he Italians make myriad different vegetable and bean soups, and each cook has her own signature combination of vegetables. Here is a vegetarian version that will have those who don't eat their vegetables begging for more. If you don't have *semi de melone*, a tiny, flat pasta that looks like melon seeds, you can cook up a batch of small pasta, such as macaroni, baby shells, or even mini penne, and stir it in at the end. ○ *Serves 6*

COOKER: Medium round or oval
SETTINGS AND COOK TIMES: LOW for 6 to 8 hours (cabbage added at 4 hours), then HIGH for 15 to 20 minutes

2 medium-size carrots, diced

3 stalks celery, chopped

2 medium-size zucchini, halved lengthwise and thinly sliced into half-moons

6 plum tomatoes, seeded and chopped, or one 14.5-ounce can fire-roasted tomatoes with their juice

One 16-ounce can cannellini beans, rinsed, drained, and half of the beans mashed

One 15-ounce can Great Northern beans, rinsed and drained

1 teaspoon salt

A few grinds of black pepper, or to taste

1 teaspoon crumbled dried mixed Italian herbs *or* 1 teaspoon dried thyme and
    ½ teaspoon dried oregano

¼ cup fresh Italian parsley leaves, chopped

Three 14.5-ounce cans low-sodium chicken broth or light vegetable broth *or*
    6 cups water plus concentrated chicken bouillon or vegetable bouillon cubes
    added per package directions

1 hard Parmesan cheese crust, 1 to 2 inches long (optional)

½ small head napa cabbage, cored and chopped or sliced into ribbons

⅓ cup *semi de melone* pasta or orzo

Extra-virgin olive oil for drizzling

Freshly grated Parmesan cheese for serving

1. Place the carrots, celery, zucchini, tomatoes, beans, salt, pepper, herbs, and broth in the slow cooker. Wipe the outside edge of the Parmesan crust clean with a damp paper towel and add it to the crock, if using. Cover and cook on LOW for 6 to 8 hours. At 4 hours, add the cabbage; cover and continue to cook on LOW.

2. When the soup is almost done, discard the Parmesan crust and add the pasta. Cover and simmer on HIGH for 15 to 20 minutes to cook the pasta.

3. Ladle the soup into serving bowls and serve hot, drizzled with olive oil and sprinkled with lots of grated Parmesan.

Using canned beans and hominy in your slow cooker soups means they will cook faster than with their dried counterparts. When done, these quick soups can sit on LOW or KEEP WARM for hours until you are ready to eat. Here are a few of my favorites.

The Simplest Black Bean Soup Ever • Serves 4

I adore this soup. It is one of my standbys since it is easy to make with pantry staples right out of the cupboard. I even carry it to a friend's for lunch right in the pot. Vary the soup's flavor by buying different jarred salsas. I look for those that have a pretty smooth texture; just make sure to use a cooked-style salsa.

COOKER: Medium round or oval
SETTING AND COOK TIME: HIGH for 2 to 4 hours

Four 15-ounce cans black beans, rinsed and drained
1 cup salsa of your choice
Two 14.5-ounce cans low-sodium chicken broth or light vegetable broth
Salt to taste
A few grinds of black pepper
¼ cup chopped fresh cilantro
1 cup (4 ounces) cubed Monterey Jack cheese, for serving
Lime or lemon wedges for serving

1. Place the beans, salsa, and broth in the slow cooker. Cover and cook on HIGH for 2 to 4 hours.

2. Puree using an immersion blender, or transfer to a food processor or blender and puree in batches. Season with salt and pepper and adjust the consistency with water or more hot broth (I like it thick).

3. Ladle into serving bowls, sprinkle with the cilantro and cheese, add a squeeze of lime or lemon juice, and serve immediately.

Posole Verde • Serves 4

During the testing of recipes for the first Not Your Mother's slow cooker book, one of my testers contributed a vegetarian posole. Well, I ended up loving it and making variations on it, like this one with tart tomatillos adapted from one of my favorite magazines, *Veggie*

Life. Posole is a whole hominy stew. Hominy is cooked, dried corn kernels that have been treated with lime; it is used dry to grind into flour for tortillas. It has a fabulous flavor and is especially nice in soups. This is one of the easiest ways to use fresh tomatillos; they have a unique, very fresh flavor and are widely available in well-stocked supermarket produce sections. Don't forget all the garnishes; they make the soup really special and more filling.

COOKER: Medium or large round or oval
SETTING AND COOK TIME: HIGH for 3 to 4 hours

1 large yellow onion, diced
3 cloves garlic, minced
1 small dried hot red chile, seeded and chopped
6 cups light vegetable broth *or* 6 cups water and 4 vegetable bouillon cubes
   (I use Rapunzel brand)
10 tomatillos, husked, rinsed, and coarsely chopped
One 4-ounce can diced roasted green chiles, drained
One 28-ounce can white or yellow hominy, drained
1 teaspoon crumbled dried oregano
¼ cup minced fresh cilantro
½ teaspoon salt, or to taste
Freshly ground black pepper to taste

GARNISHES:
Warm flour tortillas
Shredded iceberg lettuce
Sliced radishes
Chopped red onion
Crumbled feta cheese
Diced avocado
Cubed extra-firm tofu
Toasted pumpkin seeds
Chopped fresh cilantro
Lime wedges

1. Place the onion, garlic, red chile, broth, tomatillos, green chiles, hominy, and oregano in the slow cooker. Cover and cook on HIGH for 3 to 4 hours. In the last hour of cooking, add the cilantro and salt and season with pepper.

2. Serve in shallow soup bowls with warm flour tortillas and go wild with your choice of garnishes offered in separate bowls, squeezing lime juice over everything.

Tomato and White Bean Soup ● Serves 4

This is a very basic, very tasty toss-it-together-for-lunch soup. You could certainly skip the step of cooking the onion and garlic, but I like the taste so I always do it. You can add some type of small cooked pasta, like shells or farfalle bow ties (the miniature size), if you want the soup to be a bit more filling. It also tastes wonderful with a few handfuls of kale, escarole, or spinach added at the end.

COOKER: Medium or large round or oval
SETTING AND COOK TIME: HIGH for 2 to 4 hours

2 tablespoons olive oil
1 medium-size yellow onion, chopped
3 cloves garlic, pressed
Two 14.5-ounce cans plain or fire-roasted stewed tomatoes with their juice,
    crushed with your hands if tomatoes are whole
Two 16-ounce cans white beans, rinsed and drained
Two 14.5-ounce cans low-sodium chicken broth or light vegetable broth
2 tablespoons chopped fresh Italian parsley
½ teaspoon crumbled dried mixed Italian herbs
Salt to taste
A few grinds of black pepper
1 cup (4 ounces) freshly grated Parmesan cheese, for serving

1. In a small skillet, heat the olive oil over low heat, add the onion, and cook, stirring a few times, until softened, about 5 minutes. Add the garlic and cook for 30 seconds just to color the garlic slightly.

2. Combine the tomatoes and their juice, the beans, the cooked onion and oil, the broth, and the herbs in the slow cooker. Cover and cook on HIGH for 2 to 4 hours.

3. Season with salt and pepper, then ladle into large, deep soup bowls, sprinkle with plenty of Parmesan, and serve hot.

Fresh Cream of Corn Soup

T his is a summer soup, the essence of simplicity, perfect when you've just returned from the farmers' market with a whole lotta corn you couldn't resist buying. It is dairy-free and very easy to make, except for shucking and cutting the corn. Do invest in a corn zipper, which is one of the best tools ever invented to remove corn from the cob; it even gets some of the milk. I also recommend an immersion blender here, one of my favorite kitchen hand tools. Be sure to use silken tofu, which has a very soft texture. Pumpernickel rye croutons or some warm biscuits are nice with this soup. ○ *Serves 6*

COOKER: Large round or oval
SETTING AND COOK TIME: LOW for 3 to 4 hours

10 to 12 ears fresh corn, shucked and kernels cut off the cob to yield about 6 cups
1 medium-size sweet onion, finely chopped
½ teaspoon ground cumin
6 cups water or light vegetable broth
1 pound silken tofu
2 to 3 teaspoons salt, to your taste
A few grinds of black pepper
2 to 3 tablespoons extra-virgin olive oil, for drizzling
2 tablespoons minced fresh chives, for sprinkling

1. Place the corn, onion, cumin, and water in the slow cooker. Scrape the cobs for any milk and add it to the cooker as well. Cover and cook on LOW for 3 to 4 hours, until the vegetables are soft.

2. Add the tofu in chunks. Puree using an immersion blender, or transfer to a food processor or blender and puree in batches; the soup should be nice and fluffy-thick, with some whole corn left. Add the salt and pepper, stir to mix, cover, and cook on LOW for about 15 minutes to heat through.

3. Serve in shallow bowls; drizzle each bowl with olive oil and sprinkle with chives.

Cream of Carrot-Orange Soup

This soup has just a hint of curry and orange juice. The potato is added to give it body. This has an optional garnish of a fantastic homemade mango chutney, which you can make in your medium-size slow cooker while the soup is cooking in the large cooker. You will have some chutney left over; it's wonderful served alongside poultry or added to curried chicken salad (page 60). ○ *Serves 8*

COOKER: Soup, Large round or oval; Chutney, Medium round
SETTINGS AND COOK TIMES: Soup, LOW for 6½ to 8½ hours;
  Chutney, HIGH for 2 to 3 hours

2 large russet potatoes, peeled and chopped

2 medium-size yellow onions, chopped

2½ pounds carrots (about 12 medium-size), scrubbed, tops cut off, and chopped

4 cups low-sodium chicken broth

1 to 2 small cloves garlic, to your taste, pressed

¼ cup (½ stick) unsalted butter

1 heaping tablespoon honey

1 teaspoon curry powder

½ teaspoon salt, plus more to taste

⅛ teaspoon ground allspice

1 cup orange juice

3 to 4 cups half-and-half

Freshly ground black pepper to taste

SLOW COOKER MANGO CHUTNEY:

2 mangoes, peeled, pitted, and finely chopped

2 medium-size tart apples, such as Fuji, peeled, cored, and finely chopped

2 firm pears, such as Bartlett, peeled, cored, and finely chopped

½ cup firmly packed light brown sugar

1 cup finely chopped red onion

⅓ cup cider vinegar

½ teaspoon curry powder

1. Place the potatoes, onions, carrots, broth, garlic, butter, honey, curry powder, salt, and allspice in the slow cooker. Cover and cook on LOW for 6 to 8 hours, until the vegetables are soft.

2. Puree the soup using an immersion blender, or transfer to a food processor or blender and puree in batches; the soup should be nice and thick. Stir in the orange juice and 3 cups of the half-and-half; add more to achieve your desired consistency. Season with salt and pepper. Cover and cook on LOW for at least 30 minutes to heat through. Keep the soup warm on LOW until serving; don't let it come to a boil.

3. Meanwhile, place all the chutney ingredients in a medium-size slow cooker; toss to combine. Cover and cook on HIGH for 2 to 2½ hours, until the mixture reaches the desired jam-like consistency and the fruits are soft. You can have a chutney that still has little chunks of fruit, or cook it longer to make it more like a thick puree. If you want a thicker chutney, uncover and let the chutney cook for another 30 minutes to thicken to the desired consistency. Either way, when the chutney is to your liking, turn off the cooker, remove the cover if necessary, and let cool to room temperature in the crock. The chutney can be stored in an airtight container in the refrigerator for up to 2 weeks. Serve cold or at room temperature.

4. To serve, ladle the hot soup into deep bowls and top with a few tablespoonfuls of the mango chutney.

Potato-Leek-Spinach Soup

This creamy soup is sure to be a favorite. Take care to clean the leeks well under running water; there can be sand between the layers. You really don't have to worry about proportions, but I use one leek for every potato. Serve with fresh French bread. ◦ *Serves 6*

COOKER: Medium round or oval
SETTING AND COOK TIME: LOW for 5 to 7 hours, spinach added during last hour

3 medium-size leeks (white part only), root ends trimmed, washed well, and
    thinly sliced to yield about 4 cups
3 large russet potatoes, peeled and cut into chunks
5 cloves garlic
6 to 7 cups light vegetable broth or low-sodium chicken broth
12 ounces fresh spinach, tough stems removed and washed well
Salt to taste
⅓ cup crème fraîche, sour cream, or plain yogurt
¾ teaspoon freshly ground white pepper
Juice of ½ lemon
2 tablespoons unsalted butter

1. Place the leeks, potatoes, and garlic in the slow cooker. Add enough broth to cover the vegetables. Cover and cook on LOW for 5 to 7 hours, until the potatoes are tender. About an hour before the soup is done (test the potatoes; they should be getting soft), add the spinach.

2. Season with salt, then stir in the crème fraîche, pepper, lemon juice, and butter. Puree using an immersion blender, or transfer to a food processor or blender and puree in batches. Ladle the hot soup into bowls and serve immediately.

Creamy Tomato-Basil Soup

One day, my sister Meg was out shopping at the mall for Lego toys with her son Stefan and he wanted to go to lunch. They went to the Nordstrom Café, where she ordered tomato-basil soup and Stefan ordered macaroni and cheese. While waiting for his order, he wanted a taste of Meg's soup and, to her amazement, he loved it. They ended up splitting the bowl. Now every time they do their Lego shopping, Stefan requests the tomato-basil soup! Meg adapted this version from one of Nordstrom's cookbooks. It calls for two types of basil, dried and fresh. Our version is perfect paired with a tuna or grilled cheese sandwich, or alongside a burger. ○ *Serves 6*

COOKER: Large round or oval
SETTING AND COOK TIME: LOW for 8 to 10 hours, or HIGH for 4 to 5 hours; then LOW for 15 minutes

⅓ cup olive oil
1 large yellow onion, chopped
6 medium-size carrots, chopped
Three 28-ounce cans Italian plum tomatoes in puree
1 tablespoon crumbled dried basil
One 14.5-ounce can low-sodium chicken broth
2 cups heavy cream
3 tablespoons minced fresh basil
Salt and freshly ground black pepper to taste
Plain thick yogurt (preferably Greek style) or sour cream for serving

1. Combine the olive oil, onion, carrots, tomatoes with their puree, dried basil, and broth in the slow cooker. Cover and cook on HIGH for 4 to 5 hours or on LOW for 8 to 10 hours, until the carrots are soft.

2. Puree the soup using an immersion blender, or transfer to a food processor or blender and puree in batches. Stir in the cream and fresh basil, and season with salt and pepper. Cover and cook on LOW for about 15 minutes to heat through. Adjust to KEEP WARM until serving; do not let it come to a boil.

3. Ladle the hot soup into bowls and top with a dollop of cold yogurt.

Most Excellent Mushroom-Barley Soup

A friend gave me a copy of this recipe with the word "excellent" scribbled in the margin. It is a simple soup, everything going into the pot at once, except for some parsley at the end. You can make this with a combination of fresh mushrooms, like cremini and baby portobellos; they exude their juices as they cook, which flavors the soup and creates more broth. Be sure to get some really good paprika and keep it in the refrigerator (a tip from my Hungarian relatives) so it is very fresh. Also be sure to use pearl barley, not quick-cooking barley; they have different textures. ○ *Serves 4*

COOKER: Medium or large round or oval
SETTING AND COOK TIME: LOW for 6 to 7 hours

1½ pounds fresh white and/or brown mushrooms, thinly sliced
1 medium-size leek (white part only), root end trimmed, washed well, and thinly sliced
1 medium-size onion, quartered, then thinly sliced
2 tablespoons sweet Hungarian paprika
½ cup pearl barley, rinsed
One 14.5-ounce can low-sodium beef broth
One 14.5-ounce can diced tomatoes with their juice
½ cup water
2 tablespoons red wine vinegar
Salt to taste
½ teaspoon freshly ground black pepper
½ cup finely chopped fresh Italian parsley

1. Place the mushrooms, leek, and onion in the slow cooker. Sprinkle with the paprika. Add the barley, broth, tomatoes, water, and vinegar. Cover and cook on LOW for 6 to 7 hours, until the barley is tender.

2. Season with salt and pepper, then add the parsley and let stand for 10 minutes. Ladle the hot soup into bowls and serve immediately with French bread.

Roasts, Ribs, and Other Good Stuff

Tired of eating out? Had one too many stir-fries and pan-fried steaks? Pull out your slow cooker and make one of these delicious recipes for pot roast, meatloaf, ribs, burgers, and more. Many of these dishes involve braising, which is cooking a large cut of meat for a long time at a low temperature in a small amount of liquid (unlike stewing, which involves cut-up meat cooked in lots of liquid). Braising slowly breaks down tough cuts of meat and makes them tender beyond belief. It's a cooking technique tailor-made for the slow cooker.

There are four basic steps in slow cooker braising:

1. **Browning:** Brown the meat in a single layer in a skillet on the stovetop, using a bit of oil or not, over high heat to sear the surface. Don't rush this step. The more developed the color, the deeper and more concentrated the flavor of the finished dish will be.

2. **Deglazing:** After you transfer the browned meat to the slow cooker, add aromatics like garlic, shallots, and onions to the skillet and cook until softened. Wine or broth can then be added to the hot pan; bring it to a boil and scrape up any browned bits stuck to the bottom of the pan. Add more liquid, such as additional wine or broth, beer, water, tomato juice, or V8, and bring to a simmer.

3. **Slow-cooking:** Place all of the ingredients in the crock. Cook until the meat and/or vegetables are fork-tender, usually 7 to 10 hours on LOW.

4. **Finishing:** Remove the meat or vegetables from the crock, transfer to a large plate, and cover loosely with aluminum foil. Transfer the liquid from the slow cooker to a pan on the stovetop and reduce it over medium-high heat to make a delicious sauce. Alternatively, you can make the sauce by adding a slurry (cornstarch combined with water) or *beurre manié* (flour and butter kneaded together) to the hot liquid in the crock. Cook on HIGH, uncovered, for 10 to 20 minutes, until the liquid has thickened enough to barely coat the back of a spoon.

Whether you're braising or not, keep in mind these tips for cooking any kind of meat in the slow cooker:

- Keep perishable foods, such as meats and vegetables, refrigerated until prep time.

- If you decide to cut up vegetables or meats the night before you're planning to cook them, be sure to store each item in separate containers in the refrigerator.

- Purchase roasts and other large cuts of meats in a size and shape that will fit into your slow cooker. Otherwise, you'll need to trim the meat. The large oval slow cooker is one of the best sizes for all-purpose cooking of roasts.

- To end up with the least amount of fat in finished slow cooker dishes, trim your meat of any excess fat before putting it in the slow cooker. Or you can make the dish the day before, refrigerate, then skim off any congealed fat before reheating.

- Avoid using completely frozen foods in the slow cooker, since it slows the heating of the crock's contents considerably. Thaw at room temperature, in the refrigerator overnight, or in a microwave oven before adding frozen foods to the cooker.

- Do not remove the lid from the crock during the first three-quarters of the cooking time, as lots of heat will be lost and your cook time will increase. Remove the lid only to stir food as directed in a recipe or check for doneness.

•• Guide to Internal Temperatures for Meat ••

The most reliable way to tell when meat has reached a particular stage of doneness is with an instant-read thermometer or accurate meat thermometer. I recommend this tool as basic equipment for testing meat doneness in every slow cooker kitchen. Use this chart as a guide.

Type of Meat	Rare	Medium	Well-Done
Beef	125° to 130°F	140° to 145°F	160°F
Veal	Not recommended	140° to 145°F	160°F
Lamb	130° to 140°F	140° to 145°F	160°F
Pork and Ham	Not recommended	145° to 150°F	160°F

The Best Corned Beef and Cabbage

Once, on a road trip on St. Patrick's Day, I stopped in a small brewery in Hopland, California. To the side of the old standup bar serving Red Tail Ale was a small restaurant. All the food was homemade in a kitchen the size of a large broom closet. The specialty that day was corned beef (spiced by the chef) and cabbage, steamed potatoes and carrots, homemade bread, and, for dessert, grasshopper pie in a chocolate cookie crust. The meal was memorable and I have been re-creating it ever since. Corned beef is one of the most popular dishes to make in the slow cooker. ○ *Serves 6*

COOKER: Medium or large round or oval

SETTINGS AND COOK TIMES: Corned beef, LOW for 9 to 11 hours; Cabbage, HIGH for 20 to 30 minutes

6 medium-size red potatoes, quartered

4 medium-size carrots, cut into 2-inch chunks on the diagonal

1 medium-size yellow onion, cut into 6 wedges

One 3- to 4-pound corned beef brisket with seasoning packet, rinsed

3 whole cloves

½ teaspoon black peppercorns

2 teaspoons firmly packed dark brown sugar

One 12-ounce can light, dark, or nonalcoholic beer

1 medium-size head white cabbage, cut into 8 wedges, each secured with kitchen twine so it doesn't fall apart in the cooker

½ cup Dijon mustard, for serving

1. Place the potatoes, carrots, and onion in the slow cooker. Lay the corned beef on top of the vegetables and sprinkle with the seasonings from the packet, the cloves, peppercorns, and brown sugar. If the meat is too big to lay flat in your cooker, cut it in half and stack the pieces one atop the other. Add the beer and enough water to just cover the beef. Cover and cook on LOW for 9 to 11 hours.

2. Remove the corned beef from the crock and place it in on a serving dish. Arrange the vegetables around the beef; cover with aluminum foil to keep warm.

3. Place the cabbage in the slow cooker with the cooking liquid and turn the setting to HIGH. Cover and cook until crisp-tender, 20 to 30 minutes.

4. Serve the beef, sliced across the grain, with the mustard, vegetables, and cabbage, with the juices from the crock on the side.

Slow Cooker Tip: Jump-Start Your Slow-Cooking

Many cooks like to start their slow cookers on the HIGH setting for the first hour to heat up the contents of the crock more quickly, then switch back to LOW for the remainder of the cooking time.

Not Your Mother's Pot Roast with Root Vegetable Sauce

T his simple, old-fashioned pot roast is sublimely delicious, with fork-tender, succulent meat and a rich-tasting sauce of pureed vegetables. It has been adapted and improved from the pot roast recipe in my first Not Your Mother's cookbook with help from a dedicated reader. Look for a thick pot roast and, if you like, salt it with 1½ teaspoons salt the day before preparing to tenderize it. Chuck is the preferred cut for a flavorful and juicy pot roast, but other good choices are brisket, rump roast, and top and bottom round. You should make this pot roast the day before you plan to serve it. ● *Serves 4 to 6*

COOKER: Large round or oval
SETTING AND COOK TIME: LOW for 7 to 8 hours

2 tablespoons olive oil, or more as needed
½ cup finely diced carrot
½ cup finely diced celery, including some leaves
½ cup peeled and finely diced potato
1 turnip, peeled and diced
½ cup finely diced onion
One 3-pound boneless chuck roast, trimmed of as much fat as possible and blotted dry
⅔ cup dry red wine
1⅓ cups boiling water
½ teaspoon salt
¼ teaspoon freshly ground black pepper
2 pounds root vegetables, for serving, such as quartered Red Bliss potatoes,
    halved baby carrots, peeled turnips cut into wedges, and/or 1 to 2 medium-size onions,
    each cut into 8 wedges
Hot pepper sauce, such as Tabasco, for serving

1. In a large, heavy skillet, heat 1 tablespoon of the oil over medium-high heat. When hot, add the carrot, celery, potato, turnip, and onion, and cook, stirring a few times, until the vegetables have begun to soften and have browned a bit, about 5 minutes. Scrape them into the slow cooker.

2. Heat the remaining 1 tablespoon olive oil in the skillet over medium-high heat. When the oil is hot, add the meat and brown on all sides. Place the roast in the cooker on top of the vegetables.

3. Pour the wine into the skillet and raise the heat to high. As the wine boils, use a wooden spoon to scrape up any browned bits stuck to the bottom of the skillet. When the wine has reduced to a syrupy consistency, pour it over the meat along with the boiling water. Cover and cook on LOW for 7 to 8 hours.

4. Remove the meat to a covered container, scraping any clinging vegetable bits back into the cooker. Use an immersion blender and puree the vegetables and cooking liquid. Add the salt and pepper. Refrigerate the roast and sauce in separate containers overnight.

5. The next day, remove the layer of congealed fat from the sauce and any remaining fatty bits from the roast. Pour enough sauce into a large, wide saucepan or Dutch oven to cover the bottom and place the roast on top. Cook over low heat, covered, until heated through, about 1 hour.

6. Meanwhile, in a separate saucepan, heat the remaining sauce over low heat; thicken, if necessary, with a bit of potato starch slurry (I don't usually find it necessary, but you can use 1 tablespoon potato starch to 2 tablespoons water). Place the sauce in a gravy boat.

7. About 20 minutes before serving, steam the root vegetables until tender.

8. Place the roast in the center of a serving platter. Arrange the steamed vegetables around the meat and drizzle hot sauce over everything. Serve immediately, with the extra root vegetable sauce on the side.

Famous Crock Roast

Every good cook has a famous pot roast—oops, I mean crock roast. Here is one of my slow cooker favorites—rump roast cooked all day with vegetables. Rump is known for being a flavorful cut off the round (the hind leg), and it is perfect for pot roast. ○ *Serves 6*

COOKER: Large round or oval
SETTING AND COOK TIME: LOW for 8 to 9 hours, then HIGH for 15 minutes

2 tablespoons olive oil
One 3- to 4-pound boneless rump roast, trimmed of as much fat as possible and blotted dry
2 teaspoons dried thyme
Salt and freshly ground black pepper to taste
1 medium-size yellow or white onion, cut into 8 wedges
4 medium-size carrots, cut into thick slices on the diagonal
3 cloves garlic, crushed
1 bay leaf
1 cup dry red wine
½ cup low-sodium beef broth
1 tablespoon cornstarch dissolved in 2 tablespoons cold water

1. Coat the inside of the crock with nonstick cooking spray. In a large skillet, heat the olive oil over high heat, then brown the roast on all sides. Place the roast in the crock fat side up; sprinkle with the thyme and season with salt and pepper. Drizzle with the olive oil from the pan. Place the onion, carrots, garlic, and bay leaf around the sides of the roast. Pour the wine and broth into the skillet; bring to a boil and scrape up any browned bits stuck to the bottom of the pan. Pour over the roast. Cover and cook on LOW for 8 to 9 hours, until fork-tender.

2. Remove the roast to a cutting board, tent with aluminum foil, and let rest for 10 minutes. Turn the cooker to HIGH and add the cornstarch slurry to the juices in the crock. Stir a few times and simmer, uncovered, for 15 minutes to thicken. Cut the roast into thin slices and serve with the juices and vegetables from the crock.

Italian Pot Roast with Olive Oil Mashed Potatoes

Anchovies are one of the secrets of Italian cuisine, but many people seem to dislike the idea of them. When properly used with a light hand, however, no one will ever know they are in this pot roast, yet they add an important dimension of flavor. This is a simple roast and it loads into the cooker very quickly. Let it cook all day nice and slow, and enjoy it with the olive oil mashed potatoes. ○ *Serves 6*

COOKER: Large round or oval
SETTING AND COOK TIME: LOW for 7 to 8 hours

One 3-pound boneless chuck roast, trimmed of as much fat as possible, blotted dry, and cut in half crosswise
2 anchovies, cut into ½-inch pieces, or 3 cloves garlic, cut into thick slices
Salt and freshly ground black pepper to taste
1 tablespoon olive oil
1 large yellow onion, cut into 8 wedges
One 14.5-ounce can diced tomatoes, drained
1 vegetable bouillon cube, crushed
½ cup dry red wine or water

OLIVE OIL MASHED POTATOES:
2½ pounds Yukon Gold potatoes, cut in half
3 tablespoons extra-virgin olive oil
1 tablespoon unsalted butter
Salt and freshly ground black pepper to taste

1. With a sharp paring knife, cut 4 slits in both halves of the meat; stuff the slits with pieces of the anchovies or garlic. Generously season with salt and pepper. In a large skillet, heat the olive oil over medium-high heat, swirling to coat the bottom of the pan. Sear the beef until browned on all sides, about 5 minutes.

2. Coat the inside of the crock with nonstick cooking spray. Place the beef in the crock and add the onion, tomatoes, and bouillon cube. Add the wine. Cover and cook on HIGH for 7 to 8 hours, until the meat and vegetables are fork-tender.

3. Meanwhile, make the mashed potatoes. In a large saucepan, cover the potatoes with cold water, bring to a boil, reduce the heat to medium, and simmer until tender, about 20 minutes. Drain well and return to the pan on the stovetop to evaporate any extra water, if necessary. Let cool for 5 minutes, then smash the potatoes with a masher or large fork along with the olive oil and butter. Season with salt and pepper. Keep warm until ready to serve.

4. Transfer the meat to a cutting board; thinly slice against the grain and discard any gristle. Skim the fat off the top of the sauce. Serve the beef with the mashed potatoes and generously spoon the sauce over everything.

•• How Does a Slow Cooker Work? ••

Slow cooker recipes require less liquid than recipes that use conventional cooking methods because the liquid created in the slow cooking process does not evaporate as it does when cooking on the stove, on a grill, or in the oven. Slow-cooking uses "moist" cooking techniques like braising, stewing, and poaching. As the food cooks in the crock, moisture condenses and accumulates under the lid. These droplets of moisture then fall onto the food, self-basting it. The liquid will not boil away or evaporate, so, combined with the food juices, you will end up with more liquid than when you began. Don't lift the lid to check on the food during cooking; just peer in through the glass cover until you are ready to check for doneness, or else the food will take longer to cook.

You will see recipes in this book calling for 1 to 2 cups or more of liquid (stews and soups), a small amount such as ¼ cup (braising), or no liquid at all—in the last case, the natural juices exuded by the vegetables and meat will be enough to cook them perfectly.

When a recipe calls for little or no liquid, meats are placed on a bed of vegetables. This allows the vegetables direct contact with the crock so they cook faster. In addition, the meat juices will flow down onto the vegetables and help them cook, as well as add flavor.

For best results, use the slow cooker size and shape recommended in each recipe.

Beginner's Pot Roast with Mushroom Gravy and Fettuccine

Eye of round is a lean cut of beef that makes for a delicious, incredibly tender pot roast in the slow cooker. This will taste like you slaved over it all day.

○ Serves 6

COOKER: Large round or oval
SETTING AND COOK TIME: LOW for 8 to 10 hours

2 tablespoons all-purpose flour
½ teaspoon freshly ground black pepper
One 2½- to 3½-pound eye of round roast beef, trimmed of as much fat as possible and blotted dry
1 tablespoon olive oil
1 medium-size sweet yellow onion, thinly sliced
2 pounds small red potatoes, halved or quartered, depending on the size
One 1-pound bag baby carrots
One 14.5-ounce can condensed cream of mushroom soup
One 1.2-ounce package brown gravy mix (such as Knorr)
1 clove garlic, minced
½ cup water
1 pound fettuccine

1. Combine the flour and pepper in a small bowl; rub it all over the meat. In a large, heavy skillet over high heat, heat the olive oil until very hot. Sear the roast for 3 minutes on each side.

2. Coat the inside of the crock with olive oil nonstick cooking spray. Spread the onion slices over the bottom of the crock, then mix together the potatoes and carrots and place them on top of the onion. Set the seared roast over everything. In a small bowl, stir together the soup, gravy mix, garlic, and water; pour the mixture over the roast. Cover and cook on LOW for 8 to 10 hours, until the meat and vegetables are fork-tender.

3. When the pot roast is done, cook the fettuccine according to the package directions until *al dente*. Meanwhile, taste the pot roast for seasoning and adjust as needed. Remove the meat to a cutting board and thinly slice against the grain. Place the sauce from the cooker in a bowl with a ladle or in a gravy boat. Serve the roast with the fettuccine, vegetables, and gravy.

Roast Beef and Mushrooms
Braised in Barolo

Eye of round roast is Sunday food. Our family always ate Sunday dinner at around one in the afternoon. Here is an excellent version of that family meal, with a roast beef that is lean, moist, and scrumptious (and not often used in the slow cooker!). It calls for rich and gutsy Barolo red wine, known as the "king" of Italian wines and named for one of the towns in the middle of the Piedmont vineyard region; to get the authentic taste be sure to use this type of wine. You can brown the meat in a skillet before putting it in the crock if you are in the mood, but it is not mandatory. Serve with orzo pasta, polenta, or mashed potatoes. ◦ *Serves 6*

COOKER: Large round or oval
SETTING AND COOK TIME: HIGH for 4 to 5 hours

2 medium-size yellow onions, halved and thinly sliced into half-moons
One 2½- to 3½-pound eye of round roast beef, trimmed of as much fat as possible
1 teaspoon salt
A few grinds of black pepper
1 pound white mushrooms, quartered
2 cloves garlic, chopped
2 sprigs fresh thyme
Two 14.5-ounce cans diced tomatoes, drained
⅔ cup Barolo wine

1. Coat the inside of the crock with nonstick cooking spray and arrange the onions over the bottom. Rub the meat with the salt and pepper, then place on top of the onions. Arrange the mushrooms and garlic around the meat. Add the thyme, tomatoes, and wine. Cover and cook on HIGH for 4 to 5 hours, until the meat is nice and tender.

2. Discard the thyme sprigs. Transfer the roast to a cutting board and cover with aluminum foil. Let rest for 10 minutes. You can serve the roast with the crock juices as they are or transfer them to a saucepan and bring to a boil to thicken them. Cut the roast into thin slices and serve with the sauce.

Martha's Tri-Tip with Vegetables

Tri-tip roast is a great way to serve roast beef to two diners, with enough left over for another meal, roast beef sandwiches, or a cold beef salad. It comes in a size weighing 2 to 2½ pounds, perfect for small-portion cooking. Look for it at a butcher shop or well-stocked supermarket meat department. It is also delightfully economical. Tri-tip is a chunk cut off the bottom of the sirloin, so it is juicy and has a wonderful flavor. I would never have thought to cook it in the slow cooker, but Martha, my literary agent, did with fantastic results. "The tri-tip on sale at the supermarket was too appealing to pass up," wrote Martha. "It stayed in the freezer until one cold, rainy day when no one wanted to shop. This dish helped clean out the produce drawer, as well." ● *Serves 4*

COOKER: Large round or oval
SETTING AND COOK TIME: LOW for 7¾ to 8¾ hours

One 2- to 2½-pound beef tri-tip roast, fat trimmed to ¼ inch and blotted dry
¼ teaspoon salt, or to taste
Freshly ground black pepper to taste
6 medium-size boiling onions (about 6 ounces), quartered
8 ounces baby carrots
2 stalks celery, cut into 2-inch lengths
1 cup low-sodium chicken broth
1 cup frozen petite peas, thawed
Hot cooked rice for serving
Chopped fresh parsley for garnish (optional)

1. Rub all sides of the roast with the salt and pepper. Place the onions in the bottom of the slow cooker and arrange the roast on top of them. If the roast doesn't fit easily into the cooker, cut off about one-third and place it on top of the bigger piece. Add the carrots, celery, and broth. Cover and cook on LOW for 7 to 8 hours, until tender, checking at 7 hours to see if the meat shreds easily.

2. Add the peas, cover, and cook for another 45 minutes.

3. Transfer the beef to a cutting board, tent with aluminum foil, and let rest for about 10 minutes. Carve the beef and serve over rice with the vegetables and juices, garnished with parsley, if you like.

•• Homemade Barbecue Sauce ••

While barbecue sauce is considered a finishing sauce in grill cookery, slow-cooking simmers the meat right in the sauce, allowing the sauce to meld into the meat. If you don't want to use a commercial bottled barbecue sauce, here is a sauce to concoct in your slow cooker. If you plan to serve some extra sauce on the side, be sure to boil it vigorously in a saucepan in case it has come in contact with raw meat. You can double or triple this recipe; if you do, use a large cooker. ◉ Makes 3 cups

COOKER: Medium round or oval
SETTING AND COOK TIME: LOW for 5 to 6 hours

3 tablespoons olive oil
1 medium-size yellow onion, finely chopped
Three 8-ounce cans tomato sauce
½ cup red wine vinegar
½ cup firmly packed brown sugar
2 tablespoons Worcestershire sauce
1 teaspoon paprika or smoked paprika
A few drops of Tabasco sauce

1. In a small skillet, warm the oil over medium heat, then cook the onion, stirring a few times, until limp, about 10 minutes.

2. Combine the tomato sauce, vinegar, brown sugar, Worcestershire sauce, paprika, and Tabasco in the slow cooker. Add the cooked onion. Cover and cook on LOW for 5 to 6 hours.

3. If the sauce is not thick enough for you, remove the cover of the slow cooker, turn the setting to HIGH, and cook for up to 30 minutes until you achieve the desired consistency. Let the sauce cool, then transfer it to a jar and store, covered, in the refrigerator for up to 2 weeks or in the freezer for up to 3 months.

Barbecue Burgers

I got the idea for making burgers in the slow cooker from a recipe I found on the Internet. It had never occurred to me before. The burgers are shaped nice and thick, just right to fit the buns, and then stacked in the cooker. Barbecue sauce is poured over the burgers and they cook all afternoon. You'll want to serve these with toasted buns because the burgers have lots of sauce. You can make them with ground beef, turkey, or so-called meatloaf mix containing a combination of ground beef, pork, and veal. The burgers taste great cold the next day, so don't worry if there are any leftovers. ○ *Serves 8*

COOKER: Large round or oval
SETTING AND COOK TIME: LOW for 4 to 6 hours

2 pounds lean ground beef
1 large green bell pepper, seeded and finely chopped
1 medium-size onion, finely chopped
1½ cups dry Italian seasoned bread crumbs
2 large eggs, beaten
One 18-ounce bottle of your favorite barbecue sauce or 2 to 3 cups homemade
    barbecue sauce (opposite page)
12 soft hamburger buns, split and toasted

1. Place the ground meat in a medium-size bowl. Add the bell pepper, onion, bread crumbs, and eggs, and mix well, using your hands or a large fork. Be careful not to compact the meat. Divide the mixture in half. Shape each portion into 6 burgers, 1 inch thick, about the size of your bun, to make 12 burgers total. Gently arrange the burgers in the slow cooker, layering them, then pour the barbecue sauce over the burgers. Cover and cook on LOW for 4 to 6 hours, until the burgers are firm and an instant-read thermometer inserted in the center of one registers 160°F.

2. Remove each burger from the cooker with a plastic spatula and place on the toasted buns. Serve immediately, dripping with barbecue sauce.

Old-Fashioned Meatloaf with Fresh Tomatoes and Two Cheeses

My sister Meg and I agree that the best meatloaf recipes include milk-soaked bread as one of the ingredients. This is the real old-fashioned way to bind the meat. Many cooks swear that the meatloaf that emerges from a slow cooker is better than anything to come out of a traditional oven. This recipe isn't formed into a loaf, but is spread over the bottom of the slow cooker, making a flat loaf shaped like the crock. ● *Serves 4*

COOKER: Large oval
SETTING AND COOK TIME: HIGH for 3 to 3½ hours

3 slices day-old sandwich bread (about 6 ounces), crusts removed and
    bread torn into pieces
½ cup milk
2 pounds ground beef chuck *or* a combination of 1 pound ground chuck and
    1 pound ground sirloin *or* 2 pounds meatloaf mix (equal parts ground beef,
    ground pork, and ground veal)
½ cup bottled chili sauce or ketchup
2 large eggs, beaten
1 tablespoon Worcestershire sauce
½ cup minced onion
A few tablespoons of grated carrot
¼ cup minced fresh Italian parsley
Pinch of dried marjoram or mixed Italian herbs
1½ teaspoons salt
A few grinds of black pepper
4 ounces sliced Muenster cheese
4 ounces sliced mozzarella cheese
2 to 3 ripe Roma tomatoes (about 1 pound), cut into thick slices
2 tablespoons olive oil

1. Place the bread and milk in a small bowl; let soak until the bread has absorbed the milk, about 15 minutes.

2. Fold a 2-foot sheet of aluminum foil in half lengthwise; fit it into the crock, over the bottom and up the sides.

3. Squeeze the milk from the bread and place the bread in a large bowl. Add the meat, chili sauce, eggs, Worcestershire sauce, onion, carrot, parsley, marjoram, salt, and pepper. Using your hands or a large fork, mix gently but thoroughly, being careful not to compact the meat. Spread the mixture in the crock and pat into an even layer, filling out the entire bottom of the cooker. Cover with the slices of the cheese, then with the tomato slices, overlapping them. Drizzle with the olive oil. Cover and cook on HIGH for 3 to 3½ hours, until an instant-read thermometer inserted into the center of the meatloaf registers 160° to 165°F.

4. To serve, use a plastic spatula to lift out thick slices of the meatloaf. Serve hot with ketchup, or refrigerate and serve cold the next day.

Mustard Short Ribs of Beef and Meg's Twice-Baked Potato Casserole

You will need two slow cookers for this meal. The short rib recipe comes from Nancyjo Riekse, coordinator of the farmers' markets in Auburn, California. She recommends you use your favorite mustard, such as Dijon, honey, or coarse-grained; each type will vary the taste slightly. You can also use this recipe to prepare turkey legs or lamb ribs. This is served with a crockful of mashed potatoes, making it a real comfort-food meal. The ribs and potatoes both have the same cook time. ○ *Serves 4*

COOKER: Ribs, Large round or oval; Potatoes, Medium round or oval
SETTING AND COOK TIME: Ribs and Potatoes, LOW for 4 to 6 hours

4 pounds beef short ribs, trimmed of excess fat and cut into 5-inch lengths
⅓ cup mustard of your choice
2 tablespoons freshly squeezed lemon juice
1 tablespoon sugar
1 teaspoon salt
½ teaspoon freshly ground black or white pepper
2 cloves garlic, crushed
4 medium-size onions, thinly sliced

MEG'S TWICE-BAKED POTATO CASSEROLE:
3½ pounds red potatoes, quartered
¼ cup (½ stick) unsalted butter
Two 3-ounce packages cream cheese
½ cup sour cream
¼ cup whole milk or half-and-half
1 cup (4 ounces) shredded mild cheddar cheese
Salt and freshly ground black pepper to taste
Thinly sliced green onions for serving

1. Arrange the short ribs in the slow cooker, stacking them if necessary.

2. In a medium-size bowl, whisk together the mustard, lemon juice, sugar, salt, pepper, and garlic, then spread it over the ribs. Top with the sliced onions. (For the best flavor, cover and refrigerate, turning the beef occasionally, for 24 hours.) Cover and cook on LOW for 4 to 6 hours, until the meat is falling off the bone.

3. At the same time, make the potatoes. In a large saucepan, cover the potatoes with cold water and simmer over low heat until tender, about 20 minutes. Drain well and return to the pan on the stovetop to evaporate any extra water, if necessary. Add the butter, cream cheese, sour cream, milk, and ½ cup of the cheddar. Smash the potatoes with a masher or large fork to blend all the ingredients. Season with salt and pepper.

4. Lightly coat the inside of a medium-size crock with nonstick cooking spray. Spoon in the potato mixture. Sprinkle the remaining ½ cup cheddar over the potatoes. Cover and cook on LOW for 4 to 6 hours. Sprinkle with green onions right before serving.

5. Divide the ribs among 4 serving plates and serve with some mashed potatoes on the side.

Garlic-Rosemary Leg of Lamb with Tabbouleh Mint Salad

One of the surprises of the slow cooker is how well it cooks leg of lamb. But you don't just pop it whole into the slow cooker. Have your butcher bone and butterfly it, just as if you were grilling. I use the oval cooker, which fits the meat perfectly. The tabbouleh salad has lots of tomatoes and mint and goes really well with the lamb. ● *Serves 8*

COOKER: Large oval
SETTING AND COOK TIME: LOW for 6 to 8 hours

One 2- to 3-pound boneless leg of lamb, butterflied
2 tablespoons olive oil
6 stalks celery, cut into 2-inch lengths
1 large onion, coarsely chopped
4 to 5 large new potatoes, cut into large pieces
1 pound baby carrots
2 to 3 cloves garlic, minced
1 tablespoon chopped fresh rosemary or 1 sprig fresh rosemary
½ teaspoon salt
¼ teaspoon freshly ground black pepper
½ cup low-sodium chicken broth

TABBOULEH MINT SALAD:
1 cup fine bulgur
2 cups boiling water
1 bunch green onions, minced
8 ounces cucumbers, peeled, seeded, and diced
4 medium-size ripe tomatoes, seeded and chopped
½ cup minced fresh Italian parsley
½ cup minced fresh mint
⅓ cup freshly squeezed lemon juice
⅓ cup olive oil
Salt and freshly ground black pepper to taste

1. Coat the inside of the crock with nonstick cooking spray. Rub the lamb with the olive oil. Place the celery, onion, potatoes, and carrots in the crock. Arrange the lamb over the vegetables, top with the garlic and rosemary, and sprinkle with the salt and pepper. Pour in the broth. Cover and cook on LOW for 6 to 8 hours, until the lamb and vegetables are fork-tender.

2. While the lamb is cooking, make the tabbouleh. Place the bulgur in a large bowl. Add the boiling water, cover with plastic wrap, and let stand on the counter for 1 hour. Fluff with a fork. Add the green onions, cucumbers, tomatoes, parsley, and mint; toss together. In a small bowl, combine the lemon juice and olive oil; season with salt and pepper and whisk to combine. Pour over the bulgur mixture and stir with a large spoon to combine. Chill until about an hour before serving. Serve at room temperature.

3. Transfer the lamb to a cutting board and cut into 16 slices. Serve with the vegetables and juices and the tabbouleh.

Slow Cooker Tip: Multiplying Recipes

While all slow cooker recipes can be doubled and tripled, what seems like a simple process easily be thrown out of balance by the liquid proportions. Plan on some experimentation to get the dish just right. To double or triple a recipe, the general rule is to multiply the liquid by one and a half times; you can add more hot liquid at the end to adjust if necessary. When multiplying recipes, be sure you have the appropriate size cooker to accommodate the increased amounts.

Crock-Roasted Pork Tenderloin

Pork tenderloin is a star in the slow cooker. It cooks up very quickly and takes to many variations, each better than the next. I don't know what it is that transforms dry onion soup mix in the slow cooker, but it is a superb secret ingredient for cooking meat. Serve this roast with mashed potatoes and roasted acorn squash halves in fall or winter, with asparagus in spring, and with stir-fried zucchini in summer. ○ *Serves 6*

COOKER: Large oval
SETTING AND COOK TIME: LOW for 4 to 5 hours, then HIGH for 10 minutes

1 tablespoon olive oil
Two 1¼-pound pork tenderloins, trimmed of silverskin and fat and patted dry
One 1-ounce package dry onion soup mix
A few grinds of black pepper
1 cup water
½ cup dry red wine
3 tablespoons low-sodium soy sauce
2 to 3 medium-size shallots, to your taste, minced
2 tablespoons cornstarch dissolved in 2 tablespoons cold water

1. Coat the inside of the crock with nonstick cooking spray. In a large skillet over medium-high heat, warm the oil, then brown the tenderloins one at a time on all sides. Place the tenderloins in the crock, arranging them side by side. Sprinkle with the soup mix and pepper. Add the water, wine, and soy sauce. Sprinkle with the shallots. Cover and cook on LOW for 4 to 5 hours, until the pork is fork-tender.

2. Remove the pork to a serving platter, cover with aluminum foil, and let rest for 10 minutes. Turn the cooker to HIGH and add the cornstarch slurry. Stir a few times and simmer, uncovered, for 10 minutes to thicken. Cut the tenderloins into ½-inch-thick slices and serve with the sauce from the cooker.

Pork Roast with Sweet Potatoes

S ometimes for a big family meal you want to serve something a little bit different but somewhat traditional. Here's a perfect choice. Don't skip the crystallized ginger; it adds a hot, sweet note that melts and complements the moist, tender pork and sweet potatoes perfectly. Serve with cranberry sauce and a crisp green salad. ● *Serves 8*

COOKER: Large round or oval
SETTING AND COOK TIME: LOW for 8 to 10 hours, or HIGH for 4 to 5 hours

2 to 3 large sweet potatoes, peeled and cut into chunks
2 green bell peppers, seeded and chopped
3 medium-size carrots, cut into 2-inch lengths
3 small yellow or white onions, quartered
One 3½- to 4-pound rolled boneless pork loin roast, trimmed of
    fat and tied with kitchen twine
1 teaspoon crumbled dried oregano or marjoram
¼ teaspoon garlic powder
Salt and freshly ground black pepper to taste
½ cup apple cider or unfiltered apple juice
¼ cup low-sodium chicken broth
3 tablespoons brown sugar
2 tablespoons chopped crystallized ginger

1. Coat the inside of the crock with nonstick cooking spray and add the sweet potatoes, bell peppers, carrots, and onions. Rub the roast with the oregano, garlic powder, salt, and pepper; nestle the roast into the vegetables. Combine the apple cider, broth, and brown sugar; pour the liquid over the roast. Sprinkle with the crystallized ginger. Cover and cook on LOW for 8 to 10 hours or HIGH for 4 to 5 hours, until the meat is tender when pierced with the tip of a knife and an instant-read thermometer inserted into the thickest part registers 160°F.

2. Transfer the roast to a platter, cover with aluminum foil, and let stand for 10 minutes. Remove the twine and carve the roast into thick slices. Serve with the vegetables and juices from the crock.

Chinese Apricot Pork Roast with Buckwheat Soba Noodle Salad

T his is one of the easiest recipes to make, and the cooking sauce goes together in minutes using staple pantry items from the ethnic foods aisle of your supermarket. Don't skip the green onion and cilantro garnish; it really complements the flavors of the roast. The accompanying soba noodle salad tastes wonderful, is simplicity itself to prepare, and is so good even the kids will devour it. Buckwheat soba noodles are available in natural foods stores and ethnic groceries. If you don't have time to make the noodle salad, you could also serve the roast with steamed jasmine rice. ● *Serves 6 to 8*

COOKER: Medium or large oval
SETTING AND COOK TIME: HIGH for 4 to 4½ hours, or LOW for 8 to 9 hours

One 3-pound rolled boneless pork loin roast, trimmed of fat and tied with kitchen twine
One 12-ounce jar duck sauce (about ¾ cup)
1 tablespoon Asian chili-garlic sauce
1 tablespoon mirin, Shaoxing rice wine, or rice wine vinegar
1 tablespoon low-sodium soy sauce
2 teaspoons toasted sesame oil
3 cloves garlic, pressed
2 tablespoons peeled and grated or finely minced fresh ginger
4 teaspoons cornstarch

BUCKWHEAT SOBA NOODLE SALAD:
20 ounces dried buckwheat soba noodles
6 tablespoons plain sesame oil
⅔ cup rice wine vinegar
3 tablespoons low-sodium soy sauce
1½ teaspoons fine sea salt
1 teaspoon sugar
1 bunch green onions (white part and most of the green), thinly sliced

⅓ cup green onions (white part and some of the green), thinly sliced on the diagonal, for garnish

⅓ cup chopped fresh cilantro, for garnish

1. Coat the inside of the crock with nonstick cooking spray and arrange the roast inside. In a small bowl, combine the duck sauce, chili-garlic sauce, mirin, soy sauce, sesame oil, garlic, and ginger; vigorously whisk in the cornstarch (this will help thicken the sauce while cooking). Pour the mixture over the pork roast. Cover and cook on HIGH for 4 to 4½ hours or LOW for 8 to 9 hours, until the pork is fork-tender and an instant-read thermometer inserted into the thickest part registers 160°F.

2. While the pork roast is cooking, make the noodle salad. Cook the noodles in a large pot of boiling water according to the package directions until twice their size and tender to the bite, about 6 minutes. Drain in a colander and rinse with cold water. Place in a serving bowl and toss with 2 tablespoons of the sesame oil to prevent sticking.

3. In a small bowl, whisk together the remaining 4 tablespoons sesame oil, the vinegar, soy sauce, salt, and sugar. Pour the dressing over the noodles; toss to coat the noodles lightly with the dressing. Cover and chill until serving. The salad can be made up to 1 day ahead. Toss with the green onions right before serving.

4. Remove the pork from the crock to a platter and cover with aluminum foil; let stand for 10 minutes. Pour the cooking liquid into a bowl; let stand for 10 minutes, then skim any fat from the surface of the liquid. Remove the twine from the roast, then cut the pork into slices, arrange on a serving platter, then sprinkle with the green onions and cilantro. Serve the sauce on the side, gravy style, along with the noodle salad.

·· The Family of Ribs ··

The slow cooker excels at cooking ribs, a favorite summer party food. Ribs have a reputation for being messy to prepare, but the slow cooker takes care of that. No need to precook the ribs in boiling water; the slow cooker does the job perfectly with no fussy preparation. Just load up the cooker and come back when the ribs are done. While ribs cooked on a grill or roasted in an oven can be chewy, slow-cooked ribs are fall-apart tender.

Ribs are a food that cannot be cooked dry; they need a sauce and/or marinade to be properly cooked and tenderized. Ribs are naturally a bit fatty, so they stay nice and moist during the long cooking and soak up whatever sauce you braise them in. Since the slow cooker does not impart that smoky flavor from outdoor cooking or soaked wood chips, you can use a smoky-tasting barbecue sauce instead.

With pork ribs, you've got three choices: spareribs, baby back ribs, and country-style ribs. For all three cuts, buy only USDA 1 graded pork and buy fresh for the best flavor. **Spareribs** are the most popular because of their meatiness and wonderful flavor; they are cut from the lower rib cage of the animal, down by the belly, after the bacon is removed. They come in slabs of about 3 pounds, each containing 13 ribs, which is enough to feed three people. Carefully inspect your slab so you can get one with plenty of meat and the least amount of fat. You can cook your slab whole, divide it into one or two sections to stack in your round slow cooker, or divide it into individual portions.

Though very popular in restaurants, **baby back ribs** are not the meatiest ribs. A slab feeds only 1 to 2 people, so you will need to fill the slow cooker to the top to feed a group.

Country-style ribs are little loin pork chops since they are from the part of the upper rib that modulates into the loin. Often they have been butterflied or split. They have a high meat-to-bone ratio. They are very popular in the southern United States, and to most people they are the tastiest since they are so meaty. For the amount of meat they contain, they are an inexpensive choice and a favorite for braising in the slow cooker.

Beef short ribs come from the 12 ribs that traverse the lower belly area behind the brisket and just below the prime rib, so they are very tasty. Short ribs are also referred to as flanken (especially in German cookbooks). When purchasing beef ribs, figure 1 pound per person, or more if you want leftovers.

Sweet and Sour Country Ribs

T hese ribs are coated with a tasty glaze of hoisin sauce, rice wine vinegar, honey, soy sauce, and a little pineapple juice. After opening the jar of hoisin, store it in the refrigerator, where it will last nearly forever. Serve these ribs with steamed rice and a cabbage slaw. ○ *Serves 8*

COOKER: Large round or oval
SETTING AND COOK TIME: LOW for 8 to 9 hours

1 cup low-sodium soy sauce
1 cup hoisin sauce
½ cup honey
½ cup pineapple juice or papaya nectar
⅓ cup rice wine vinegar
¼ cup peanut or sesame oil
2 tablespoons chopped garlic
8 pounds country-style pork spareribs, cut into serving pieces of 3 to 4 ribs

1. In a large bowl, combine the soy sauce, hoisin sauce, honey, pineapple juice, vinegar, oil, and garlic. Add the ribs and turn to completely coat them with the marinade. Cover and refrigerate for 1 to 2 hours.

2. Arrange the rib portions in the slow cooker and pour the marinade over them. If you are using a round cooker, lift the ribs so the sauce can get in between them. Cover and cook on LOW for 8 to 9 hours, until the meat is tender and starts to separate from the bone. Serve immediately, with lots of napkins.

Barbecue Pork Ribs

This is a down-and-dirty entertaining recipe at its tastiest. Pick up your favorite commercial barbecue sauce and add a few pantry items for a fabulous meal. Eight pounds of ribs will be about four full slabs. Serve these ribs with baked beans and potato salad. ○ *Serves 8*

COOKER: Large round or oval
SETTING AND COOK TIME: LOW for 8 to 9 hours

8 pounds pork spareribs, cut into portions of 3 to 4 ribs
4 cups barbecue sauce of your choice, store-bought or homemade (page 118)
1 cup ketchup
2 tablespoons Worcestershire sauce
¼ cup firmly packed brown sugar

1. Arrange the rib portions in the slow cooker. Combine the barbecue sauce, ketchup, Worcestershire sauce, and brown sugar in a large bowl and mix until smooth; spoon over the ribs. If you have a round cooker, lift the ribs so the sauce can get in between them. Cover and cook on LOW for 8 to 9 hours, until the meat is tender and starts to separate from the bone.

2. If extra sauce remains on the bottom of the cooker, place it in a bowl and serve on the side. Serve the ribs immediately, with lots of napkins.

Honey-Glazed Ham

ou can choose a precooked ham of any type and cook it nicely in your slow cooker. I adore the taste of ginger ale in cooking, especially with pork.

Serves 6 to 10

COOKER: Large oval
SETTING AND COOK TIME: LOW for 6 to 8 hours

One 4-pound boneless cooked ham
One 12-ounce can just-opened ginger ale
½ cup honey
¼ cup firmly packed brown sugar
½ teaspoon ground cloves
½ teaspoon dry mustard

1. Coat the inside of the crock with nonstick cooking spray. Place the ham in the crock and pour the ginger ale over it. Cover and cook on LOW for 3 hours.

2. Combine the honey, brown sugar, cloves, and mustard in a small bowl with about ¼ cup of the hot liquid from the crock; stir. Spoon over the ham; cover, and continue cooking on LOW until an instant-read thermometer inserted in the thickest part registers at least 165°F, another 3 to 5 hours.

3. Remove the ham from the cooker to a platter. Cover with aluminum foil until serving. Slice the ham and serve hot with the crock juices. Let any leftovers come to warm room temperature, wrap tightly, and refrigerate.

Great-Tasting Dinners on the Wing

You can prepare most every type of chicken in the slow cooker—the whole bird, breasts, thighs, drumsticks, or wings. If you are cooking chicken parts, it is most often worth the extra step of browning them on the stovetop first to give an additional punch of flavor to the final dish. Cooking chicken parts with the skin on (you can remove it before serving) will help keep the chicken from drying out. Figure on about 8 ounces meat per serving with bone-in chicken and 4 to 6 ounces per serving for boneless.

A Cornish game hen is a young, small chicken, weighing no more than 2 pounds, sold whole. One game hen will serve 1 or 2 people, depending on their appetites.

Turkey, which is especially suited to the slow cooker, is available whole, in parts (drumsticks, wings, halved or whole breasts, and thighs), ground, and as bone-in and boneless breast roasts—all of which are good for slow-cooking except for the whole turkey, which is too large to fit in the cooker. Plan on one pound of meat per person for bone-in turkey, 12 ounces per person for boneless.

Use very little liquid when cooking poultry in the slow cooker—much less liquid than you would use in stovetop or oven cooking. Generally speaking, 1/2 to 3/4 cup of liquid is plenty. If you want a thick, richly flavored sauce to serve with your poultry dish, you can reduce the cooking liquid on the stovetop, perhaps thickening it with a cornstarch slurry or *beurre manié* (kneaded butter) before serving. This takes only a few minutes and is well worth the time.

Safe Poultry Practices

Thaw poultry in the refrigerator in its original wrapping with a plate underneath to catch any drips. It is important that the bird remain cold while thawing. A whole bird takes about 24 hours per 5 pounds to thaw; parts will thaw in 12 hours. Refrigerate cooked poultry within two hours of cooking, never letting it come to room temperature before refrigerating. Never buy frozen poultry that has frozen liquid in the package, which indicates it was frozen after sitting for a while or was refrozen. Poultry will keep in the freezer for a maximum of 9 to 10 months.

Because poultry may carry potentially harmful organisms or bacteria, take care when handling it. Thoroughly wash the poultry and dry it before beginning to work with it. Wash your hands, work surfaces, and utensils with hot soapy water before and after handling. Poultry should always be cooked completely through, never rare like beef and lamb. Slow-cooking is an excellent method to thoroughly cook poultry of all types.

Slow Cooker Poultry Pointers

- Cook poultry that has been handled and stored properly. Fresh poultry needs to be stored in the refrigerator until preparation time and cooked within 1 to 2 days to minimize bacterial growth. Before cooking, rinse it thoroughly with cold water and pat dry. Either load the slow cooker immediately with the raw poultry, or precook as directed in the recipe and place the poultry into the cooker immediately after browning.

- Since the slow cooker takes a few hours to reach a safe bacteria-killing temperature, transfer the poultry directly from the refrigerator to the cooker and get the cooker turned on quickly. Please note the danger zone for bacterial growth in poultry is between 40° and 140°F. The heating rate for a slow cooker is 3 to 4 hours on the LOW setting to get the contents up to a safe food temperature of 140° to 165°F; it will then increase to over 200°F by 6 hours. The same temperatures will be reached in half the amount of time on the HIGH setting. We recommend that you do not lift the lid of the slow cooker during the first 3 to 4 hours of cooking to allow the heat inside to come to the proper cooking temperature as quickly as possible.

- Never use room-temperature poultry. Unless a recipe specifically calls for it, never place frozen poultry directly into the slow cooker, as it will take much longer for it to reach a safe cooking temperature than defrosted refrigerated poultry.

- Smaller poultry pieces cook more efficiently than large pieces or a whole bird. Boneless pieces, such as breasts and thighs, cook the fastest, with bone-in pieces taking longer. Please add time, 1 to 2 hours, if substituting bone-in poultry for boneless in a recipe, or follow the instructions in a recipe designed for the type of poultry you are using.

- Poultry should be cooked throughout but still be juicy (the juices should run clear when tested with a knife). While poultry has both white and dark meat, when properly cooked there will be no trace of pink when pierced with a fork at the thickest point. Poultry is done when the internal temperature reaches about 160°F for white meat or 170°F for dark on an instant-read thermometer, an invaluable tool when cooking meat in the slow cooker.

Fastest Chicken with Mole Sauce

Mole poblano is one of Mexico's most famous dishes. It is dark brown in color, due to the addition of chocolate, with a toasty, smoky, sweet-hot flavor. Whenever you eat it, the sauce is unmistakable. Making mole sauce from scratch is a major undertaking since it has a long list of ingredients and fresh chiles to prepare, but you don't have to do that in order to eat mole at home. Just look for mole pastes or concentrates in the ethnic foods section of your supermarket (Doña Maria is one brand that is easy to find). You simply mix the paste or concentrate with chicken broth or water and pour it over the chicken in the crock. If you like a sweeter mole, add a disk or two of Ibarra or bittersweet chocolate to the mole. Steam fluffy white or brown rice, heat up a can of black beans, toast some sesame seeds, and you are good to go! ○ *Serves 4*

COOKER: Medium or large round or oval
SETTING AND COOK TIME: HIGH for 3 to 3½ hours

4 boneless, skinless chicken breast halves (about 1½ pounds), rinsed, patted dry,
    and trimmed of fat
1 tablespoon light olive oil
1 large yellow onion, chopped
One 8.25-ounce jar mole poblano concentrate
Two 14.5-ounce cans low-sodium chicken broth
2 cups hot steamed rice, for serving
One 15-ounce can black beans, rinsed, drained, and heated in the microwave, for serving
1 cup sour cream (low-fat is okay), crumbled cojita cheese, or
    shredded Monterey Jack cheese
2 tablespoons sesame seeds, toasted in a dry skillet for a few minutes until golden
¼ cup chopped fresh cilantro

1. Coat the inside of the crock with nonstick cooking spray and arrange the chicken in the crock.

2. In a medium-size skillet over medium-high heat, warm the olive oil, then cook the onion, stirring a few times, until softened, about 5 minutes. Transfer to a blender or food processor, add the mole and broth, and blend until smooth. Pour the mixture over the chicken. Cover and cook on HIGH for 3 to 3½ hours, until the chicken is tender and cooked through. Check for doneness at 3 hours.

3. Serve the chicken fanned over the rice and beans, topped with a dollop of sour cream or sprinkling of cheese, the toasted sesame seeds, and cilantro.

Slow Cooker Tip: Using the Stoneware Insert

The slow cooker crock, but not the lid, can also be used as ovenware. Cover the crock with foil, if necessary, during baking. Do not use the slow cooker crock in the microwave or on the stovetop, unless the manufacturer's instructions for your machine say that you can do so. Do not refrigerate cooked food in the crock; it will not cool down fast enough to chill the contents properly. Always transfer the food to covered containers before storing in the refrigerator.

Tarragon Chicken in Mushroom Sauce with Simply Delicious Oven-Baked Rice

One of my slow cooker cooks, Marty Brewer of Mountain View, California, emailed me the following note about this successful slow cooker dish she had made: "Well, my slow cooker recipe result was dee-lish and a huge hit with everyone! And s-o-o-o-o easy. I also served a rice casserole (which came from a wonderful binder-type book I got years ago at a hospital in Truckee—*Sierrandipity: A Sierra Cookbook*—put out by the Tahoe Forest Hospital auxiliary). Salad was layered slices of zucchini, tomato, and onion with an olive oil and lemon dressing. Bread was crescent rolls (from a tube) spread with a butter and Parmesan mixture before rolling and shaping." I was ready for dinner just reading her description. If you are a cheese fan, you can place slices of Swiss cheese over the chicken and cook for 8 minutes or so on HIGH to melt it. ● *Serves 8*

COOKER: Large round or oval
SETTING AND COOK TIME: LOW for 4 to 4½ hours

16 to 24 chicken breast tenders, rinsed and patted dry
8 boneless, skinless chicken thighs (about 2 pounds), rinsed, patted dry, and trimmed of fat
12 ounces white mushrooms, sliced
2 cloves garlic, slivered
¼ cup (½ stick) unsalted butter
One and a half 10.75-ounce cans condensed cream of chicken soup
¾ cup dry sherry
2 teaspoons Worcestershire sauce
1 teaspoon crumbled dried tarragon

OVEN-BAKED RICE:
1½ cups raw long-grain white rice
Three 10.5-ounce cans condensed chicken broth
1½ cups chopped celery
½ cup chopped onion
½ cup (1 stick) unsalted butter, cubed
Chopped fresh Italian parsley for serving

1. Coat the inside of the crock with butter-flavored or olive oil nonstick cooking spray. Add the chicken, mushrooms, and garlic in separate layers.

2. In a medium-size saucepan or microwave-safe bowl, combine the butter, soup, sherry, Worcestershire sauce, and tarragon; whisk until smooth and heat just until hot. Pour the mixture over the chicken. Cover and cook on LOW for 4 to 4½ hours, until the chicken is tender and cooked through.

3. While the chicken is cooking, prepare the rice. Preheat the oven to 350°F. Combine the rice, broth, celery, onion, and butter in a covered casserole dish. Bake until the rice is tender and all the liquid is absorbed, about 1 hour.

4. Sprinkle the rice with the chopped parsley and serve alongside the creamy chicken.

Braised Chicken Breasts
on a Bed of Vegetables

My friend Bunny Dimmel whips up this chicken any day of the week, loving the combination of onion, garlic, and peppers. You can also use bone-in breast halves or two turkey thighs, both of which will take a bit longer to cook. For chicken that is not smothered in a sauce or liquid, it is best to cook it for a short time on HIGH rather than longer on LOW to keep the meat from becoming stringy.

○ *Serves 4*

COOKER: Large round or oval
SETTING AND COOK TIME: HIGH for 3 to 3½ hours

2 large white or sweet onions, sliced

4 cloves garlic, slivered

2 large red bell peppers, seeded and sliced into ½-inch-thick strips or rings

1 large green bell pepper, seeded and sliced into ½-inch-thick strips or rings

4 boneless, skinless chicken breast halves (about 1½ pounds), rinsed, patted dry, and trimmed of fat

½ cup water or low-sodium chicken broth

1 lemon, halved

2 tablespoons olive oil or 2 tablespoons unsalted butter cut into pieces

A few grinds of black or white pepper

1. Coat the inside of the crock with butter-flavored or olive oil nonstick cooking spray. Arrange the onion slices in the bottom of the cooker. Sprinkle with the garlic, then arrange the bell peppers on top. Place the chicken breasts on top of the vegetables; pour in the water. Squeeze the juice from the lemon halves over the breasts, then drizzle with the olive oil or dot with butter and sprinkle with the pepper. You can leave the lemon halves in the crock, if you like, for some extra flavor. Cover and cook on HIGH for 3 to 3½ hours, until the chicken is tender and cooked through. Check for doneness at 3 hours.

2. When the chicken is cooked, remove it with tongs from the crock and place on dinner plates. Serve with lots of the vegetables and the juices from the crock spooned over the chicken and some steamed brown rice or whole-wheat couscous.

Slow Cooker Cacciatore

A t one time, the entire continent of Europe was a vast forest and many meat dishes were prepared hunter-style, *alla cacciatora*, with tomatoes and garlic in a deep kettle over an open fire outdoors or in a fireplace. Chicken cacciatore recipes appear in Hungarian and Polish cookbooks, as well as Italian ones. This recipe is from my sister Amy, who considers cacciatore her favorite dinner; she makes it with chicken thighs and drumsticks. ◦ *Serves 4*

COOKER: Medium or large round or oval
SETTINGS AND COOK TIMES: HIGH for 2½ to 3 hours, or LOW for 6 to 7 hours; then 10 to 15 minutes on HIGH to thicken the sauce

2 cups prepared marinara sauce or homemade tomato sauce
1 medium-size yellow onion, halved and thinly sliced into half-moons
1 to 3 cloves garlic, to your taste, minced
1 large green bell pepper, seeded and cut into 1½-inch pieces
1 pound boneless, skinless chicken thighs (about 4), rinsed, patted dry, and trimmed of fat
4 chicken drumsticks, skin removed, rinsed, and patted dry
6 ounces white mushrooms, quartered
2 tablespoons all-purpose flour or instant flour (such as Wondra)
2 tablespoons water
2 tablespoons dry white wine

1. Coat the inside of the crock with butter-flavored or olive oil nonstick cooking spray. Spread half of the marinara sauce in the crock, and add the onion, garlic, bell pepper, and chicken pieces. Sprinkle the mushrooms on top and cover with the remaining marinara sauce. Cover and cook on HIGH for 2½ to 3 hours or LOW for 6 to 7 hours, until the chicken is tender and cooked through.

2. Using tongs, remove the chicken to a warm serving platter. Whisk together the flour, water, and wine until smooth. Set the cooker to HIGH and stir the flour mixture into the hot sauce until smooth. Cover and cook for 10 to 15 minutes, until thickened. Pour the sauce and vegetables over the chicken pieces and serve.

Thai-Style Chicken Thighs

This recipe makes use of basic pantry items for a quick dinner that is astoundingly good. It is adapted from a recipe in a fabulous, and little known, slow cooker cookbook, *Pillsbury Doughboy Slow Cooker Recipes* (Clarkson Potter, 2003). Serve over steamed long-grain white rice with lots of chopped cilantro.

○ *Serves 4*

COOKER: Medium or large round or oval
SETTING AND COOK TIME: HIGH for 3 to 3½ hours

2½ pounds boneless, skinless chicken thighs (about 8), rinsed, patted dry,
 and trimmed of fat
1 cup salsa of your choice
¼ cup smooth peanut butter
2 tablespoons low-sodium soy sauce
One 2- to 3-inch piece fresh ginger, peeled and grated
¼ cup chopped dry-roasted peanuts, for garnish (optional)
¼ cup chopped fresh cilantro, for garnish

1. Coat the inside of the crock with nonstick cooking spray and arrange the chicken in the crock. In a small bowl, stir together the salsa, peanut butter, soy sauce, and ginger until well combined; pour over the chicken. Cover and cook on HIGH for 3 to 3½ hours, until the chicken is tender and cooked through.

2. Serve the chicken from the crock with plenty of sauce, garnished with a sprinkling of peanuts, if using, and the cilantro.

Apricot-Ginger Chicken Legs

My sister Meg created this recipe on a Super Bowl weekend when she wanted something that tasted like an appetizer but would be substantial enough for a meal. It is lip-smacking good, with a coating of apricot jam and orange marmalade. To make it a meal, serve it on top of fluffy white rice. ● *Serves 6 to 8*

COOKER: Large round or oval
SETTING AND COOK TIME: HIGH for 2½ to 3 hours

2 to 4 tablespoons olive oil
4 pounds chicken legs or bone-in thighs, skin removed, rinsed, patted dry,
    and sprinkled lightly with salt
¾ cup apricot preserves
½ cup orange marmalade
¼ cup low-sodium soy sauce
1 tablespoon sesame oil
2 cloves garlic, pressed
3 medium-size shallots, finely chopped
1 teaspoon peeled and grated fresh ginger
About 2 tablespoons sesame seeds, for garnish
1 bunch green onions (white part and some of the green), chopped, for garnish

1. Coat the inside of the crock with butter-flavored or olive oil nonstick cooking spray.

2. In a large skillet over medium-high heat, warm 2 tablespoons of the olive oil. Add the chicken in batches (adding more oil as needed, 1 tablespoon at a time) and brown, turning once or twice and transferring the chicken to the crock as it browns.

3. In a medium-size bowl, combine the preserves, marmalade, soy sauce, sesame oil, garlic, shallots, and ginger with a fork. Pour the mixture over the chicken. Cover and cook on HIGH for 2½ to 3 hours, until the chicken is tender and cooked through.

4. Remove the chicken with tongs from the crock and place on dinner plates or a large platter. Serve sprinkled with the sesame seeds and green onions.

Maple Barbecue Chicken Wings

I like a sweet and sticky barbecue sauce on chicken wings. Use a bit more barbecue sauce if you want to have extra to sop up with crusty French bread. The wings can be browned first, as in this recipe, or piled into the crock without browning (but they will take a bit longer to cook if not browned first). Kids love these chicken wings for lunch or dinner with some canned baked beans on the side.

o Serves 4 as a main dish, 10 as an appetizer

COOKER: Large round or oval
SETTING AND COOK TIME: HIGH for 2 to 3 hours

4 pounds chicken wings, cut into joints, with bony wing tips reserved for stock or
    discarded, or 3 pounds chicken drumettes, rinsed and patted dry
2½ cups barbecue sauce of your choice, store-bought or homemade (page 118)
1 cup pure maple syrup, Grade B if possible

1. Coat the inside of the crock with nonstick cooking spray.

2. Preheat the broiler. Rinse the wings and pat dry. Place them on a baking sheet and broil in batches, if necessary, to brown the wings nicely, 3 minutes per side. As they brown, transfer to the crock.

3. In a large bowl, stir together the barbecue sauce and maple syrup. Pour the sauce over the wings; stir to coat evenly. Cover and cook on HIGH for 2 to 3 hours, until the chicken is tender and cooked through. If possible, stir gently halfway through cooking with a wooden spoon, bringing the wings on the top to the bottom to coat them with the sauce.

4. Serve hot or warm with lots of napkins and something cold to drink.

Mustard-Glazed Chicken Wings with Sweet and Sour Dipping Sauce

Sometimes a dinner of chicken wings and rice is just what you want. This recipe is adapted from one in an advertisement for Smucker's jam.

Serves 4 as a main dish, 10 as an appetizer

COOKER: Large round or oval
SETTING AND COOK TIME: HIGH for 2 to 3 hours

⅔ cup grainy mustard
¼ cup olive oil
1 teaspoon salt
½ teaspoon freshly ground black pepper
¼ teaspoon cayenne pepper
4 pounds chicken wings, cut into joints, with bony wing tips cut off and reserved for stock or
    discarded, or 3 pounds chicken drumettes, rinsed and patted dry

SWEET AND SOUR DIPPING SAUCE:
2 cups apricot preserves
½ cup cider vinegar
¼ cup firmly packed light brown sugar
2 teaspoons dry mustard
1 teaspoon ground ginger

1. Coat the inside of the crock with butter-flavored or olive oil nonstick cooking spray. In the crock, combine the mustard, olive oil, salt, black pepper, and cayenne with a wooden spoon. Add the wings to the crock and toss with a spoon to coat them with the mustard mixture. Spray the wings lightly with some olive oil spray. Cover and cook on HIGH for 2 to 3 hours. If possible, stir gently halfway through the cooking time, bringing the wings on the top to the bottom to coat with sauce.

2. Combine the dipping sauce ingredients in a microwave-safe bowl. Microwave on High power for 2 minutes to melt the brown sugar and preserves.

3. Serve the wings hot with the warm dipping sauce on the side.

Whole Chicken Stuffed with Rice and Golden Raisins

U nlike a roasted chicken made in the oven, slow-cooked whole chicken will not have a crisp skin, even if you do not add any liquid to the cooker. Don't fret about this: Just remove the skin and discard it. Do this after cooking so that the skin can protect the chicken flesh and keep it moist during cooking. I use a white and wild rice blend from Trader Joe's, but you can use your own combination. This is adapted from my friend Lou Pappas's book *Extra-Special Crockery Pot Recipes* (Bristol Publishing, 1994). Lou browns her chicken first, which you can certainly do if you have the time. ○ *Serves 4*

COOKER: Large oval
SETTING AND COOK TIME: LOW for 7 to 8 hours

1½ cups raw mixed long-grain white and wild rice blend, cooked according to
    package directions until barely tender
⅓ cup golden raisins
One 3- to 4-pound chicken
¾ to 1 teaspoon salt, to your taste
½ teaspoon freshly ground black pepper
2 tablespoons cold unsalted butter, thinly sliced
Zest of 1 lemon, removed with a vegetable peeler and chopped
½ cup dry white wine or low-sodium chicken broth

1. Fluff the rice in the pan and mix in the raisins; set aside. Wash and pat dry the chicken thoroughly. Reserve the giblets and neck for another use, or discard them. Sprinkle the chicken with the salt and pepper on all sides and inside the cavity. Lift the skin with your fingers and place the butter pieces flat against the flesh, then add some of the lemon zest. Sprinkle the remaining lemon zest inside the cavity and spoon in the rice; do not pack. Use a skewer to close up the cavity.

2. Place the chicken in the slow cooker, breast side up. Add the wine. Cover and cook on LOW for 7 to 8 hours, until an instant-read thermometer inserted at the thickest part of the thigh registers 170°F. The chicken is done when the juices run clear, with no trace of pink, when punctured at the thigh with a fork.

3. Transfer the chicken to a platter and remove the rice stuffing to a covered bowl to keep warm. Pour the liquid from the crock into a gravy separator and strain off the fat. Carve the chicken and serve at once with the rice, passing the juices in a gravy boat.

Crock-Roasted Chicken with Rotisserie-Style Rub and Edamame Succotash

Love rotisserie chicken? Well, with this flavorful rub, you can make your own in the slow cooker. Fresh green soybeans, called edamame and found in the frozen food section, are a great addition to succotash, where they substitute for the traditional lima beans. ● *Serves 4*

COOKER: Medium or large oval
SETTING AND COOK TIME: HIGH for 3½ to 4½ hours, or LOW for 6 to 7 hours

One 3½-pound chicken
2 teaspoons paprika
2 teaspoons chili powder
2 teaspoons kosher or fine sea salt
1 teaspoon onion powder
½ teaspoon cayenne pepper
½ teaspoon garlic powder (not garlic salt)
½ teaspoon celery salt
½ teaspoon freshly ground black pepper

EDAMAME SUCCOTASH:
1½ cups frozen shelled edamame
1 tablespoon canola oil
½ cup chopped red bell pepper
¼ cup chopped onion
2 cups fresh corn kernels (from 4 ears)
3 tablespoons dry white wine or water
2 tablespoons rice wine vinegar
2 tablespoons chopped fresh Italian parsley
2 tablespoons chopped fresh basil
Salt and freshly ground black pepper to taste

1. Rinse and pat dry the chicken, then pull off and discard any lumps of fat. Reserve the giblets and neck for another use, or discard them. Coat the inside of the crock with nonstick cooking spray.

2. In a small bowl, combine the paprika, chili powder, kosher salt, onion powder, cayenne, garlic powder, celery salt, and black pepper. Add warm water by the teaspoonful, stirring well after each addition, to make a thick paste. Using your hands, coat the chicken inside and out with the seasoned paste. Place the chicken in the crock, breast side up. Cover and cook on HIGH for 3½ to 4½ hours or LOW for 6 to 7 hours, until an instant-read thermometer inserted in the thickest part of the thigh registers 170°F. The chicken is done when the juices run clear, with no trace of pink, when punctured at the thigh with a fork.

3. Remove the chicken to a platter. Pour the liquid from the crock into a gravy separator and strain off the fat.

4. Meanwhile, make the succotash. Cook the edamame in a large saucepan of lightly salted water until tender, about 4 minutes, or according to package directions. Drain well. Heat the canola oil in a large nonstick skillet over medium heat. Add the bell pepper and onion; cook, stirring frequently, until they start to soften, about 2 minutes. Stir in the corn, water, and edamame. Cook, stirring frequently, for 4 minutes. Remove from the heat and stir in the vinegar, parsley, and basil. Season with salt and pepper.

5. Carve the chicken and serve at once with the hot succotash, passing the juices from the crock in a gravy boat.

Cornish Game Hens with Cornbread Stuffing and Sweet Potatoes

Here is a basic recipe for crock-roasting game hens. It was created by my friend Mary Cantori on one of her yearly camping trips. Cooked in a Dutch oven over a live fire, the dish was so delicious, she made it in the slow cooker immediately upon returning home. Mary makes her own cornbread for the stuffing, but I have substituted packaged stuffing mix. ● *Serves 4*

COOKER: Large oval
SETTING AND COOK TIME: LOW for 6 to 7 hours

2 tablespoons unsalted butter
½ cup chopped onion
½ cup chopped celery
One 6-ounce package cornbread stuffing mix
1 medium-size apple, peeled, cored, and chopped
½ cup chopped fresh cilantro
¼ cup dried cranberries
1 to 2 tablespoons chopped fresh sage, to your taste
½ cup low-sodium chicken broth, plus more if needed
2 Cornish game hens, rinsed and patted dry
Salt and freshly ground black pepper to taste
1 to 2 tablespoons olive oil
2 medium-size sweet potatoes, peeled and cubed

BALSAMIC-PEACH SAUCE:
1½ cups low-sodium chicken broth
½ cup peach preserves
2 tablespoons balsamic vinegar
¼ teaspoon garlic powder
Pinch of cayenne pepper

1. Melt the butter in a skillet over medium heat until it sizzles, then add the onion and celery and cook, stirring a few times, until softened, about 5 minutes. Place the dry stuffing mix in a large bowl and add the onion mixture, apple, cilantro, cranberries, sage, and enough broth just to moisten; mix with a large spoon or your hands. Coat the inside of the crock with nonstick cooking spray and spread half of the stuffing over the bottom.

2. Split each game hen in half: Place each bird, breast side up, on a cutting surface. Holding the bird with one hand and using kitchen shears with the other, cut the breast in half, starting from the neck end. Turn the bird over and cut down both sides of the backbone, as close to the bone as possible, leaving two halves; discard the backbone or use for soup stock. Season the hen halves with salt and pepper.

3. In a large skillet over medium-high heat (you can use the same skillet you cooked the onions in), heat 1 tablespoon of the olive oil, then sear the game hens on the skin side, about 2 minutes (you may need to do this in two batches; add the remaining 1 tablespoon oil if necessary). Arrange the hens overlapping, bone side down, on top of the stuffing, then pack the remaining stuffing around one side of the hens. Place the sweet potatoes around the other side. Cover and cook on LOW for 6 to 7 hours, until the hens and potatoes are tender and an instant-read thermometer inserted in the thickest part of the thigh registers 170°F. The juices should run clear, with no trace of pink, when the thigh is pierced with a knife.

4. Meanwhile, make the sauce. Place the broth in a small saucepan and bring to a boil. Stir in the preserves, vinegar, garlic powder, and cayenne; reduce the heat to low and simmer for 5 minutes.

5. To serve, place half of a hen on each dinner plate, along with some stuffing and sweet potatoes, with some sauce spooned over all.

Braised Turkey Legs

urkey legs cook beautifully in the gentle heat of the slow cooker, becoming tender and savory yet remaining moist and flavorful. This recipe provides one turkey leg per person, but if the legs you use are large, you might wish to carve the meat off the bone, in which case this should serve six. Serve with mashed carrots and potatoes mixed together. ○ *Serves 4*

COOKER: Medium or large, oval preferred
SETTING AND COOK TIME: HIGH for 2 to 3 hours

3 tablespoons olive oil
4 turkey legs *or* 2 turkey legs and 2 turkey thighs (about 4 pounds), rinsed and patted dry
1 large onion, chopped
1 large carrot, sliced
3 to 4 stalks celery, sliced
½ cup dry white wine
½ cup low-sodium chicken broth
¾ teaspoon salt
¼ teaspoon freshly ground black pepper
A few pinches of poultry seasoning
1 tablespoon cornstarch dissolved in ¼ cup water
2 tablespoons heavy cream or 1 tablespoon unsalted butter (optional)
Chopped fresh Italian parsley for garnish (optional)

Slow Cooker Tip: Taking Care of Your Crock

Get in the habit of coating the inside of the crock with nonstick cooking spray (I usually use a vegetable oil or olive oil spray) before making a recipe to prevent sticking and to facilitate easy washing of the crock. The sprays seem to work better than butter or oil, which tend to burn around the edges of the crock.

1. In a large, heavy skillet, heat the oil over medium-high heat. Brown the turkey pieces on all sides, 2 to 3 minutes per side. As the legs are browned, remove them with tongs and place them on a plate.

2. Add the onion, carrot, and celery to the skillet and cook, stirring a few times, until softened, about 5 minutes. Transfer the vegetables to the slow cooker, then place the turkey legs on top. Add the wine to the hot pan. Cook, stirring to scrape up any browned bits stuck to the bottom of the pan, until the wine has reduced a bit, 2 to 3 minutes, then add the broth. Pour the mixture over the turkey. Sprinkle with the salt, pepper, and poultry seasoning. Cover and cook on HIGH for 2 to 3 hours, until the turkey is tender. An instant-read thermometer inserted into the thickest part should register 170°F and the juices should run clear, with no trace of pink.

3. Transfer the turkey to a baking dish and place the dish in a preheated 325°F oven to keep warm while you finish the sauce. Strain the liquid from the crock into a small saucepan. Bring it to a boil over high heat and boil for 4 to 5 minutes to re-duce the sauce and concentrate the flavors. Stir in the cornstarch slurry and cook until thickened, about 2 minutes. Stir in the cream or butter, if using, until the cream is hot or the butter just melts.

4. Serve the turkey, on or off the bone, with the sauce on the side. Garnish with fresh parsley, if desired.

Old-Fashioned Turkey Breast with Pan Gravy and Cranberry-Orange Sauce

Turkey breast is lean, so keeping it moist can be a challenge, but not with the slow cooker. Here you cook the breast in a simple braising liquid and serve it with a flavorful gravy made from the juices in the crock. If you have a second slow cooker, consider making a stuffing (pages 212 and 214) for a festive meal. And don't skip this cranberry sauce, which can be made up to three weeks in advance; I got the recipe from Dolores Kostelni, known as The Happy Cook and one of my favorite radio interviewers. Use bags of fresh cranberries within two weeks of purchase so they don't get mushy or shriveled. If you use frozen cranberries, don't bother to defrost them, but plan on an extra 30 to 45 minutes in the cooker. ○ *Serves 8*

COOKER: Turkey breast, Large oval; Cranberry sauce, Medium round or oval
SETTINGS AND COOK TIMES: Turkey breast, HIGH for 4½ to 6 hours; Cranberry sauce, HIGH for 1 hour, then LOW for 2 to 3 hours

One 14.5-ounce can low-sodium chicken broth
2 cups water
2 stalks celery, cut into large pieces
1 medium-size onion, coarsely chopped
¼ cup (½ stick) unsalted butter, cut into pieces
1 teaspoon of your favorite dried mixed-herb seasoning, such as a salt-free blend like Mrs. Dash or Parsley Patch
One 5- to 6-pound bone-in whole turkey breast, rinsed and patted dry

THE HAPPY COOK'S CRANBERRY-ORANGE SAUCE:
One 12-ounce bag fresh or frozen cranberries, rinsed and picked over if fresh
¾ cup sugar
½ cup orange juice
¼ cup water
¼ to ½ cup combination of chopped dried apricots, candied ginger, and Craisins, to your taste
Grated zest of 1 navel orange

PAN GRAVY:

¼ cup instant flour (such as Wondra)

¼ cup cold water

2 to 3 tablespoons Madeira, to your taste

Salt and freshly ground black pepper to taste

1. Bring the broth and water to a boil in a saucepan on the stovetop or in a bowl in the microwave. Place the celery, onion, butter, and herb seasoning in the slow cooker. Set the turkey, breast side down, in the cooker and pour in the hot liquid. Cover and cook on HIGH for 4½ to 6 hours. The turkey is done when an instant-read thermometer inserted into the thickest part registers 160°F.

2. Meanwhile, in another slow cooker, prepare the cranberry sauce. Combine the cranberries, sugar, orange juice, and water; cover and cook on HIGH for 1 hour.

3. Crack the lid of the cooker holding the cranberry sauce and prop it open with the handle of a wooden spoon, then set the cooker to LOW and cook for another 2 to 3 hours. During the last hour, stir in the dried fruit. When cooked, the cranberries will have popped open; stir in the orange zest. Remove the lid and let the sauce cool in the crock to room temperature. The cranberry sauce will keep, tightly covered, in the refrigerator for up to 3 weeks. Serve chilled or at room temperature.

4. When the turkey is cooked, transfer it to a platter, tent with aluminum foil, and let stand for 10 minutes before carving.

5. Meanwhile, to prepare the gravy, strain the liquid left in the cooker from cooking the turkey through a cheesecloth-lined colander; press to squeeze any juice from the vegetables and discard the vegetables. Skim any fat off the strained liquid with a spoon. Pour the strained, defatted liquid into a large nonstick skillet and bring to a boil. In a small bowl, whisk together the flour, cold water, and Madeira until the flour dissolves. Pour the slurry into the skillet with the hot broth, stirring constantly with a whisk until the gravy bubbles and thickens. Season with salt and pepper.

6. Serve the hot turkey with plenty of gravy and the cranberry sauce.

Barbecue Turkey Thighs with Root Vegetables

Turkey thighs cook beautifully in the slow cooker, yet I have not seen very many recipes using them. The meat from turkey thighs is a bit tougher than chicken-thigh meat, so it holds up nicely in the slow cooker, emerging moist beyond belief. You can serve this dish with rice or noodles or with fresh country bread.

○ Serves 4

COOKER: Medium or large round or oval
SETTING AND COOK TIME: LOW for 8 to 9 hours

2 bone-in turkey thighs (1½ to 2 pounds), skin removed, rinsed, and patted dry
3 small white boiling onions, quartered
4 large new potatoes, such as White Rose or Yukon Gold, each cut into 8 wedges
4 medium-size carrots, cut in half across, then into matchsticks

BLACKBERRY BARBECUE SAUCE:
¾ cup ketchup
¼ cup seedless blackberry preserves
2 tablespoons red wine vinegar
2 tablespoons cider vinegar
1 tablespoon Worcestershire sauce
1 tablespoon brown sugar
A few pinches of cayenne pepper or chili powder
⅛ teaspoon dry mustard
¼ cup hot water

1. Coat the inside of the crock with nonstick cooking spray. Place the turkey thighs in the crock, then add the onions, potatoes, and carrots.

2. In a microwave-safe bowl, combine the ketchup, preserves, vinegars, Worcestershire sauce, brown sugar, cayenne, and mustard. Place in the microwave and heat to melt the preserves. Pour the mixture over the vegetables and turkey in the crock. Add the hot water. Cover and cook on LOW for 8 to 9 hours.

3. Remove the turkey from the crock and pick the meat off the bones; discard the bones. Shred the turkey meat and return to the crock. Stir to combine well with the sauce and vegetables. Serve in soup bowls.

Satisfying Stews and Comforting Chilis

The slow cooker was made for stew. Meat stews should always be cooked at a low simmer, never boiled, to fully develop their character and flavor, a process that is performed to perfection in the slow cooker. I recommend that you use a fattier cut of meat, such as beef chuck or veal shoulder, when making stew, as it will cook to luscious softness in the slow cooker, while a lean cut may turn stringy and tough. This is a great time to take a look at cuts of meat you might not usually give a second glance to, such as those listed on page 167.

Beef stews and braises keep for up to 3 days in the refrigerator, taste great made a day or two in advance and reheated, and can be frozen for up to 3 months. Many cooks make their stews the day before and chill them, which allows any fat in the cooking liquid to congeal on top, making it easy to remove the fat before serving.

How to Build a Better Stew

- Make sure that any hard vegetables, such as potatoes and carrots, are cut into pieces of similar size for even cooking.

- Make sure meat is also cut into uniform-size pieces for even cooking.

- Unless instructed otherwise, brown meat in a heavy Dutch oven or skillet first, then add it to the crock. Next brown onions and any other vegetables called for in the recipe, then add liquid to the skillet and deglaze the pan. Deglazing gives the liquid a deep color and rich taste. Bring the liquid to a boil before pouring it over the meat.

Home-Style Beef Stew with Orange Peel

This is a wonderful stew originally created for CorningWare back in the 1980s by Cornelius O'Donnell, who worked for Corning and was an expert on cooking in glass. He wrote a monthly magazine column and a cookbook aptly titled *Cooking with Cornelius: The Corning Cookbook* (Random House, 1982). This is his beef stew adapted for the slow cooker. ◦ *Serves 8*

COOKER: Large round or oval
SETTING AND COOK TIME: HIGH for 4 to 5 hours, or LOW for 7 to 8 hours

One 3-pound lean boneless chuck roast or round steak, trimmed of fat and cut into
   1½-inch chunks
Salt and freshly ground black or white pepper to taste
4 tablespoons olive oil
3 tablespoons all-purpose flour
2 cloves garlic, minced
3 medium-size yellow onions, chopped
4 medium-size carrots, diced
1 medium-size turnip, peeled and diced
4 strips (each about 3 inches long and 1 inch wide) orange peel, cut with a vegetable peeler
1 bay leaf
4 cups low-sodium beef broth

1. Coat the inside of the crock with nonstick cooking spray.

2. Sprinkle the chunks of beef with salt and pepper. In a large skillet over medium to medium-high heat, heat 2 tablespoons of the olive oil until very hot. Brown the meat in 2 batches, using 2 tablespoons olive oil for each batch; brown the meat on all sides, 4 to 5 minutes. As the meat is browned, transfer it to the crock.

3. Sprinkle the meat in the crock with the flour and toss to coat. Add the garlic, onions, carrots, turnip, orange peel, and bay leaf. Add the broth; mix well. Cover and cook on HIGH for 4 to 5 hours or LOW for 7 to 8 hours, until the meat is fork-tender.

4. Season with salt and pepper and serve the stew over noodles or rice, or with nice fresh bread. Leave the juices thin and ladle over the meat.

Chianti and Cherry Beef Stew

My sister Meg adapted this from a stew recipe in one of her favorite local cookbooks, published by the Junior League of Seattle. The original recipe calls for unsweetened dried cherries, but since they are not easy to find, she used sweetened dried cherries and omitted the sugar in the original recipe. You can use tart or sweet dried cherries interchangeably. Chianti is a hearty, dry red wine produced in Italy from a combination of grape varieties, and its flavor is not reproduced in any other wine, so please try to find Chianti for this stew to get the best flavor. Look for the identifying mark of the black rooster, the *gallo nero*, a sign of authenticity and quality. Serve this stew with buttered egg noodles. ● *Serves 6*

COOKER: Large round or oval
SETTING AND COOK TIME: LOW for 8 to 10 hours

3 tablespoons all-purpose flour
1¼ teaspoons salt, plus more to taste
½ teaspoon ground allspice
¼ teaspoon ground cinnamon
½ teaspoon freshly ground black pepper, plus more to taste
2½ pounds beef top loin, cut into 2-inch chunks
4 tablespoons olive oil
1 clove garlic, pressed
3 medium-size onions, cut in half and thinly sliced into half-moons (to make about 3 cups)
¾ cup dried cherries
2 tablespoons red wine vinegar
1 cup Chianti
1 cup low-sodium beef broth
8 ounces white or brown mushrooms, quartered

1. Coat the inside of the crock with nonstick cooking spray.

2. Combine the flour, salt, allspice, cinnamon, and pepper in a large zipper-top plastic bag. Add the beef, seal, and shake to evenly coat the meat. In a large skillet, heat 3 tablespoons of the olive oil and add half of the beef; cook until browned on all sides, about 5 minutes. Transfer the meat to the crock and repeat with the second batch.

3. Add the remaining 1 tablespoon olive oil to the pan. Add the garlic, onions, cherries, and vinegar; cook until the onions are light brown, being careful not to let them burn, stirring a few times. Add the mixture to the crock, then add the Chianti, broth, and mushrooms; stir to combine. Cover and cook on LOW for 8 to 10 hours, until the meat is fork-tender.

4. Season with salt and pepper and serve the stew over buttered egg noodles with plenty of the sauce.

Beef Stew Classico with Herbed Cheese Mashed Potatoes

This is a down-home, nothing fancy, mom's-style beef stew with lots of veggies. If you have never cut your own stew meat, please give it a try. You will be rewarded with tender, juicy, top-notch flavor. Get a nice chuck roast and cut it into cubes; it is that easy. Many people just toss the meat into the crock *au blanc* style, without taking time for stovetop browning, but that extra step adds immeasurable flavor to the final stew. My sister Meg's husband loves her herbed cheese mashed potatoes. She has created several versions of these using different types of potatoes, but the reds work the best; they mash up nicely and taste great. After mashing, keep them in the cooker so the cheese melts and blends in well. Yum! ● *Serves 6*

COOKER: Stew, Large round or oval; Potatoes, Medium round
SETTINGS AND COOK TIMES: Stew, HIGH for 4 to 5 hours, or LOW for 7 to 8 hours;
Potatoes, KEEP WARM for 30 minutes to 2 hours after cooking on stovetop

One 2½- to 3-pound lean boneless chuck roast, trimmed of fat and cut into 1½-inch chunks
Salt and freshly ground black or white pepper to taste
3 tablespoons olive oil
2 large yellow onions, chopped
One 1-pound bag baby carrots
2 medium-size parsnips, peeled and diced
4 cups low-sodium beef broth
1½ cups dry red wine of your choice
6 tablespoons tomato paste (I use an imported brand that comes in a tube)
10 oil-packed sun-dried tomatoes, drained and chopped
1½ teaspoons crumbled dried thyme or marjoram

MASHED POTATOES:
3 pounds red potatoes
5 tablespoons unsalted butter
½ cup sour cream
½ cup milk or half-and-half
One 5.2-ounce package garlic-herb Boursin cheese
Salt and freshly ground black pepper to taste

¼ cup (½ stick) unsalted butter, softened, or 4 tablespoons beef broth
¼ cup all-purpose flour
1 cup frozen petite peas, thawed

1. Sprinkle the chunks of beef with salt and pepper. In a large skillet over medium to medium-high heat, heat 1½ tablespoons of the oil until very hot. Add half the meat to the skillet and brown on all sides, 4 to 5 minutes. Transfer the meat to a plate. Repeat with the remaining 1½ tablespoons oil and remaining meat.

2. Coat the inside of the crock with nonstick cooking spray and add the onions, carrots, and parsnips. Add the browned meat, broth, wine, tomato paste, sun-dried tomatoes, and thyme; mix well. Cover and cook on HIGH for 4 to 5 hours or LOW for 7 to 8 hours, until the meat is fork-tender.

3. While the stew is cooking, make the mashed potatoes. Place the potatoes in a large saucepan, cover with water, and bring to a boil. Reduce the heat to a simmer and cook until the potatoes are fork-tender, about 25 minutes; drain. Add 4 tablespoons of the butter, the sour cream, milk, and Boursin and, using a potato masher or large fork, mash the potatoes to blend the ingredients well, keeping the mixture chunky. Season with salt and pepper. Transfer the potatoes to another slow cooker and top with the remaining 1 tablespoon butter, cut into pieces. Cover and leave in the cooker on KEEP WARM for at least 30 minutes and up to 2 hours, until ready to serve.

4. In a small bowl with a fork, knead together the softened butter and flour; set aside in the refrigerator. (If you don't want to use butter, stir the flour into the 4 tablespoons of broth.) During the last half hour of cooking time for the stew, add the butter-flour mixture (known as *beurre manié*) and stir until melted. Add the peas. Cover and cook for another 20 minutes, until thickened a bit. Season with salt and pepper and serve the stew with the mashed potatoes.

Sirloin Beef Stew

This beef stew is unusual in that it uses sirloin steak instead of chuck or round steak stew meat. Oh my, is it good! It is adapted from a recipe I found on one of my favorite recipe blogs, Karina's Kitchen, which is devoted to gluten-free cooking. It was Karina's son who suggested using the more expensive sirloin. Karina says, "Cover and let the magic happen. The aromas emanating from our little *cocina* drove us crazy till dinnertime. The flavors should be balanced, warm, and inviting. And he was right—the texture and flavor were melt-in-your-mouth tenderosity." Serve this with Corn Kernel Corn Muffins (page 191). ◦ *Serves 4*

COOKER: Large round or oval
SETTING AND COOK TIME: HIGH for 4 to 5 hours

2 pounds boneless top sirloin steak, cut into 2-inch chunks
Fine sea salt to taste
3 tablespoons light olive oil
4 cloves garlic, chopped
1 medium-size yellow onion, diced
4 large Yukon Gold potatoes, peeled and diced
3 large carrots, cut into ½-inch-thick rounds
3 stalks celery, sliced ½ inch thick
1 cup dry red table wine
4 cups low-sodium beef broth
2 tablespoons balsamic vinegar
1 teaspoon crumbled mixed dried Italian or French herbs, or to taste
   (a combination of thyme, sage, rosemary, and/or basil, or *herbes de Provence*)
1 bay leaf
Freshly ground black pepper to taste

1. Coat the inside of the crock with nonstick cooking spray.

2. Season the beef with salt. Warm the olive oil in a large skillet over high heat. Add the beef, in batches, and brown quickly on all sides, about 5 minutes. Using a slotted spoon, transfer the meat to the crock as it browns.

3. Add the garlic, onion, potatoes, carrots, and celery to the crock, then the wine, broth, vinegar, herbs, bay leaf, and pepper. Cover and cook on HIGH for 4 to 5 hours, until the meat is fork-tender. Serve hot.

•• The Best Cuts of Meat for Slow Cooker •• Stews and Chilis

When a recipe calls for a certain type of meat (beef, lamb, pork, or veal), you can use any of the cuts under each heading below interchangeably.

Beef
- Chuck blade roast or chuck 7-bone roast
- Boneless chuck roast
- Chuck arm steak
- Top round tip roast
- Bottom round steak
- Top sirloin steak
- Beef cheeks

Lamb
- Lamb shoulder
- Leg of lamb
- Lamb sirloin

Pork
- Boneless pork shoulder
- Pork blade roast
- Neck (purchase 1 pound per person before cutting off the bone)

Veal
- Bone-in blade roast
- Veal shoulder roast

Hearty Beef and Veal Stew

S tevie Yvaska is newsroom coordinator at the *San Jose Mercury News* and reports on the intricacies of antique furniture for the Home section. He is also a slow cooker enthusiast. "I don't brown the meat with flour," say Stevie. "This saves on the calories and, of course, with the cleanup—no frying pan to wash. I mix all of the ingredients right in the crock. That's what I love about these gizmos—no muss, no fuss. I adore the aroma you get throughout the house as the flavors meld during cooking. It's so comforting." This stew has plenty of herbs plus new potatoes, turnips, and rutabagas, the stalwarts of the winter kitchen. Serve the stew with black bread or buttered biscuits. ● *Serves 6*

COOKER: Large round or oval
SETTING AND COOK TIME: LOW for 6 to 7 hours

2 pounds lean stew beef, such as chuck or bottom round, trimmed of fat and cut into 1-inch chunks

12 ounces veal stew meat or veal shoulder, trimmed of fat and cut into 1-inch chunks

1 medium-size turnip, peeled and chopped

1 medium-size rutabaga, peeled and chopped

8 small or 4 medium-size red or Yukon Gold potatoes, chopped

1 large yellow onion, cut in half and sliced into half-moons ½ inch thick

2 small stalks celery, cut into thick slices

3 cloves garlic, pressed

4 bay leaves (can be tied in cheesecloth for easy removal)

2 tablespoons chopped fresh Italian parsley

½ teaspoon crumbled dried thyme

½ teaspoon crumbled dried tarragon

½ teaspoon crumbled dried rosemary

A few grinds of black pepper

One 12-ounce can V8 vegetable juice or tomato juice

⅔ cup dry vermouth

1. Coat the inside of the crock with nonstick cooking spray. Add the meat and all the vegetables and herbs to the crock, sprinkle with the pepper, and toss to combine. Add the V8 and vermouth; the liquid will just cover all the ingredients. Cover and cook on LOW for 6 to 7 hours, until the meat and vegetables are tender.

2. Discard the bay leaves. Serve the piping-hot stew in shallow bowls with an oversize spoon and fork.

Slow Cooker Tip: A Cool Tip for the Slow Cooker

Utilizing your freezer in conjunction with the slow cooker to make large batches is a practical way to increase your cooking efficiency. If you have the freezer space, you can cook double the amount of a favorite dish and package half for a future meal. Use plastic freezer containers and zipper-top plastic freezer bags in sizes that will hold the amount of food you plan on serving later.

The best slow cooker recipes for freezing include meat braises, pasta casseroles mixed with sauce, pasta sauces, stews, and soups. Plan to reheat your leftovers in the oven or microwave, since the slow cooker will not heat the food as quickly as necessary for food safety.

Do not freeze raw potatoes, cooked soft vegetables (such as summer squash), cream sauces, cooked poultry on the bone, fish, or hard-cooked eggs. Also avoid freezing veal, since it is so lean, risotto (plain steamed rice can be frozen nicely, though), and polenta. These foods do not retain their flavor and texture well after freezing.

Garden Lamb Stew

One of my favorite Italian cooks is San Francisco's Rick O'Connell. I took a cooking class from her in the late 1980s and once I had enjoyed her pumpkin minestrone, osso buco, and rigatoni casserole, I knew we were culinarily simpatico. When she published her cookbook, *365 Easy Italian Recipes* (HarperCollins, 1991), I was in heaven. Here is one of her recipes, adapted for the slow cooker. It is a simple stew recipe that Rick inherited from her mother. Serve it over buttered orzo pasta or rice. ◦ *Serves 6*

COOKER: Large round or oval

SETTING AND COOK TIME: LOW for 6 to 8 hours; green beans, basil, and parsley added halfway through cooking time

3 pounds lamb stew meat or lamb shoulder, trimmed of fat and cut into 1½-inch chunks

Salt and freshly ground black or white pepper to taste

¼ cup olive oil

2 cloves garlic, chopped

1 large white onion, chopped

1 cup water

One 14.5-ounce can diced tomatoes with their juice

1 pound green beans, ends trimmed and snapped in half

2 heaping tablespoons chopped fresh basil

2 heaping tablespoons chopped fresh Italian parsley

1. Coat the inside of the crock with nonstick cooking spray.

2. Season the lamb with salt and pepper. Warm the olive oil in a large skillet over high heat. Add the lamb, in batches, and brown quickly on all sides, about 5 minutes. Using a slotted spoon, transfer the lamb to the crock as it browns.

3. Add the garlic and onion to the pan and cook, stirring, until softened just a bit, about 1 minute. Add the cooked vegetables to the crock along with the water and tomatoes. Cover and cook on LOW for 6 to 8 hours, until the meat is fork-tender. Halfway through the cooking time, add the green beans, basil, and parsley. Serve hot.

Slow Cooker Tip: Save Electricity While You Cook!

The slow cooker is user-friendly and very economical, utilizing about the same amount of energy on the HIGH setting as a 75-watt light bulb. It takes much less electricity to use a slow cooker than a conventional gas or electric oven. It is an excellent alternative method of cooking on extremely hot days when energy alerts recommend reduced use of electrical appliances, with the added benefit that it won't add heat to your kitchen like an oven does.

Cinnamon Lamb Stew
with Carrot Couscous

This simple lamb stew is one of the great slow cooker meals. Here you'll find a whisper of the sweet spices associated with North African and Middle Eastern cooking. Once you find out how easy it is to make couscous, you'll prepare it often. This stew is especially appealing to young diners. ❍ *Serves 6*

COOKER: Large round or oval
SETTING AND COOK TIME: LOW for 8 to 9 hours

2 tablespoons olive oil
2 tablespoons unsalted butter
3½ pounds boneless lamb (shoulder or leg of lamb), trimmed of fat and
    cut into 1½-inch chunks
2 large onions, chopped
2 tablespoons all-purpose flour
1 cup low-sodium chicken broth or light vegetable broth
One 28-ounce can plum tomatoes, drained and chopped
1 teaspoon ground cumin
One 3-inch cinnamon stick
½ teaspoon ground cardamom
1⅓ cups golden raisins
3 tablespoons chopped fresh cilantro
Salt and cayenne pepper to taste

CARROT COUSCOUS:
2 tablespoons olive oil
1 medium-size shallot, minced
¾ cup shredded carrot
2 cups light vegetable broth
1 cup canned chickpeas, rinsed and drained
1⅓ cups instant regular or whole-wheat couscous

1. In a large nonstick skillet, heat the oil and butter together over medium-high heat until the butter sizzles. Add the lamb, in batches, and brown on all sides, 4 to 5 minutes. Transfer to the slow cooker.

2. Add the onions to the hot pan and cook until softened, about 5 minutes, stirring a few times. Sprinkle with the flour and stir. Add the broth and bring to a boil; pour the mixture over the meat in the slow cooker. Add the tomatoes, cumin, cinnamon, cardamom, and raisins. Cover and cook on LOW for 8 to 9 hours, until the lamb and vegetables are very tender.

3. Discard the cinnamon stick. Stir in the cilantro and season with salt and cayenne. Let stand while making the couscous.

4. In a medium-size saucepan, heat the olive oil over medium heat; add the shallot and carrot and cook, stirring a few times, until softened, about 5 minutes. Add the broth and bring to a boil. Add the chickpeas and couscous; stir to combine. Remove from the heat. Cover and let stand until the couscous is tender, 5 to 10 minutes.

5. Serve the stew hot with the couscous on the side in the same shallow bowl.

Plum Good Pork Stew with Ginger

One of the delights in the world of canned fruit is whole purple plums. They are often a seasonal item, so keep looking until you find them, then buy a few cans. This is a delicious pork stew, sweet and rich with fruit. I've adapted the recipe from one by Elaine Bell, a well-known caterer in the Napa Valley; at the time this recipe appeared in a food magazine in 1990, she was culinary director at Sterling Vineyards. Serve with basmati rice. ○ *Serves 4*

COOKER: Large round or oval

SETTING AND COOK TIME: LOW for 7 to 9 hours; plums and apricots added halfway through cooking time

1 large yellow onion, cut into 8 wedges

2 cloves garlic, minced

½ cup all-purpose flour

½ teaspoon salt

¼ teaspoon freshly ground white pepper

2 pounds boneless pork shoulder, trimmed of fat and cut into 1½-inch chunks

3 tablespoons olive oil

2 cups dry red wine, such as Chianti or Zinfandel

One 2-inch piece fresh ginger, peeled and grated

½ teaspoon dried orange peel or 2 teaspoons finely grated orange zest

½ teaspoon ground nutmeg

¼ teaspoon red pepper flakes

¼ teaspoon ground allspice

1 bay leaf

One 16-ounce can whole purple plums, drained (syrup reserved), pitted, and chopped

¾ cup (3 ounces) chopped dried apricots

1. Coat the inside of the crock with nonstick cooking spray. Place the onion and garlic in the crock.

2. Place the flour, salt, and pepper in a large zipper-top plastic bag. Pat the meat dry with paper towels and toss in the bag with the flour to coat. In a large skillet over medium-high heat, warm 1½ tablespoons of the olive oil until very hot. Add half the meat and cook until browned on all sides, 4 to 5 minutes. Using a slotted spoon, transfer the pork to the cooker. Repeat with the remaining 1½ tablespoons oil and the remaining pork.

3. Add the wine to the skillet and bring to a boil, scraping up any browned bits from the bottom of the pan. Add the ginger, orange peel, nutmeg, red pepper flakes, allspice, and bay leaf and stir to warm the mixture. Pour the mixture over the vegetables and meat in the cooker. Cover and cook on LOW for 7 to 9 hours. About halfway through the cook time, add the plums and their syrup and the apricots. Cover and cook until the pork is fork-tender.

4. Remove the bay leaf and discard. Serve hot.

Chicken and Sweet Potato Stew with Garlic Bread

Chicken stews are far less common than meat stews but are just as delicious. I found a recipe for this stew online and reduced the amount of potatoes to be more in proportion with the chicken and mushrooms. You simply layer the ingredients in the crock and dinner is a few hours away. Look for O brand champagne vinegar; it is widely available and modestly priced for such a luxurious flavor.

○ *Serves 6*

COOKER: Large round or oval
SETTING AND COOK TIME: LOW for 5 to 6 hours

10 boneless, skinless chicken thighs, trimmed of fat
1½ pounds sweet potatoes, peeled and cut into spears
8 ounces white or brown mushrooms, thinly sliced
6 large shallots, cut in half
3 cloves garlic, cut in half
2 sprigs fresh rosemary
Salt to taste
½ teaspoon freshly ground black pepper
One 14.5-ounce can low-sodium chicken broth
⅓ cup dry sherry

GARLIC BREAD:
¾ cup (1½ sticks) unsalted butter, softened
4 cloves garlic, minced or pressed
1 long country loaf or thick baguette, cut in half horizontally
Paprika for sprinkling

2 tablespoons champagne vinegar

1. Coat the inside of the crock with nonstick cooking spray and arrange the chicken on the bottom. Lay the sweet potatoes, mushrooms, shallots, and garlic over the chicken. Lay the rosemary on top and season with salt and the pepper. Pour the broth and sherry over the contents of the crock. Cover and cook on LOW for 5 to 6 hours, until the potatoes are fork-tender.

2. Meanwhile, make the garlic bread. Preheat the broiler. In a small bowl, mash together the butter and garlic with a fork. Spread the garlic butter evenly on the cut sides of the bread and sprinkle lightly with paprika. Place on a baking sheet and broil until browned, about 3 minutes; cut into thick portions.

3. Remove the rosemary from the crock and discard. Stir in the vinegar and adjust the seasonings if necessary. Serve the stew in shallow bowls with a fork and over-size spoon, with the hot garlic bread on the side.

Spiced Vegetable Stew with Almonds and Currants

O ne of my girlfriends gave me this favorite recipe of hers. The spices are added with a light hand for subtle but delicious flavor. Serve with warm pita bread and brown rice. ○ *Serves 4 to 6*

COOKER: Large round or oval
SETTING AND COOK TIME: LOW for 8 to 9 hours

2 tablespoons olive oil
1 cup slivered blanched almonds
3 cloves garlic, minced
1 teaspoon ground coriander
1 teaspoon ground cumin
½ teaspoon cayenne pepper
¼ teaspoon ground cinnamon
1 large globe eggplant, cut into 1-inch-thick slices, salted, and patted dry after 30 minutes
1 large yellow onion, diced
3 medium-size zucchini, cut into thick rounds
1 medium-size head cauliflower, broken into florets
Two 14.5-ounce cans stewed tomatoes with their juice
One 15-ounce can chickpeas, rinsed and drained
¾ cup dried currants
Two 14.5-ounce cans low-sodium chicken broth or light vegetable broth
Salt to taste
Plain sesame oil for drizzling
1 cup (8 ounces) plain thick yogurt (preferably Greek style) or sour cream, for serving

1. In a small skillet, heat the olive oil over medium heat. Add the almonds. Stir until the almonds are toasted, then add the garlic, coriander, cumin, cayenne, and cinnamon. Cook for 30 seconds to warm the spices.

2. Coat the inside of the crock with nonstick cooking spray and add the almond mixture, scraping the pan with a spatula. Cut the eggplant slices into fat cubes. Place the eggplant, onion, zucchini, cauliflower, tomatoes, chickpeas, and currants in the cooker. Stir to combine, then add the broth. Cover and cook on LOW for 8 to 9 hours, until the vegetables are tender but still hold their shape.

3. Season with salt, then serve the stew with a drizzle of sesame oil and a spoonful of yogurt on top.

•• Fresh Beans for Chili from the Slow Cooker ••

While most of the recipes for chili in this chapter call for canned beans, nothing can compare to the taste of fresh-cooked dried beans. There are many more types of beans to choose from if you take the time to cook them fresh. The slow cooker is one of the premier methods for cooking beans (even Julia Child used to cook her beans overnight in a slow cooker). There is no risk of burning; the slow cooker's heat is just a dash lower than the lowest setting on your stovetop, which makes for tender beans. Be careful not to overcook them, however, as beans can get mushy (though if they do, they're still good to eat in a soup). For beans that will go into a chili that will cook for a few hours, you will ideally cook them until *al dente* rather than totally soft.

There are lots of beans that can be used interchangeably in chili. The white varieties, all very different in appearance, include chickpeas (also called garbanzos or *ceci*), navy beans, baby white beans (sometimes known as *haricots*), Great Northerns, black-eyed peas, yellow-eyed peas, soybeans, and cannellini. Most of these take about 3 hours to cook in the slow cooker, except for chickpeas and soybeans, which take about 4 hours.

The rose-pink to red-black varieties include many favorite chili beans: black beans (also called *frijoles negros* or turtle beans), pintos (nicknamed "the Mexican strawberry" because of their mottled coloring) and their hybrids (such as rattlesnake and appaloosa beans), red kidneys, small pink beans (also called *pinquito*, meaning small kidney), anasazi beans, red beans, Jacob's cattle beans, and cranberry beans (also called borlotti or brown beans). These all take about 3 hours to cook.

There are a few tips for cooking beans. You can cook the beans completely plain, or flavor them by adding a *bouquet garni* (a bundle of bay leaf, celery, and an herb); a single fresh or dried chile pepper (cut an X on the bottom of the chile and add whole for a dash of flavor); or a sprig or two of fresh herbs (sage or even epazote if you find it in your ethnic grocery) to flavor your beans. Add hot water (very hot to boiling) to the dried beans, then cover and cook on the HIGH heat setting. Do not add salt until *after* the beans are cooked; salt added at the beginning toughens beans and prevents them from absorbing water properly during the cooking process. Remember that beans and legumes always take slightly longer to cook at higher altitudes.

Here are the guidelines for substituting fresh-cooked beans for canned beans in a recipe: A 15-ounce can of beans, drained, contains about 1½ cups of beans. A 16-ounce can of beans, drained, contains about 1¾ cups of beans. A 19-ounce can of beans, drained, contains about 2 cups of beans. One pound of dried beans (about 2½ cups) will yield about 5 cups of cooked beans. Cooked beans can be stored in individual zipper-top plastic freezer bags or storage containers in the freezer for up to 3 months. ❍ ½ cup dried beans yields 1 to 1½ cups cooked beans; ¾ cup dried beans yields 1¾ to 2¼ cups cooked beans; 1 cup dried beans yields 2½ to 3 cups cooked beans, depending on the size and age of the beans

COOKER: Medium round or oval
SETTING AND COOK TIME: HIGH for about 3 hours (the time will be the same for
a small amount of beans as for a large pot)

½ cup dried beans and 2½ cups boiling water *or* **¾ cup dried beans and**
3¼ cups boiling water *or* **1 cup dried beans and 4 cups boiling water**
Fine sea salt to taste (optional)

1. Place the beans in a colander and rinse under cold running water; pick over for small stones. If you would like to soak the beans, place them in the slow cooker, cover with cold water, and let them soak for 4 hours or overnight. (This is good if your beans are old, but you do not have to soak the beans to get a good pot of beans from the slow cooker.) Drain and return the beans to the crock.

2. Add the boiling water to the beans in the slow cooker. Cover and cook on HIGH until the beans are tender but still hold their shape and are not falling apart, about 3 hours. Most of the cooking liquid will be absorbed, but the beans should not be dry; you want them covered with liquid at all times, so add more boiling water if the beans start to look dry. I test for doneness at 2½ hours. The best way to test is to bite into one. You want a more *al dente* parcooked bean if you are going to add it to a chili recipe that will cook for another few hours, so plan accordingly. You can add salt now, or not, depending on how you want to use the beans. You can store the beans in the refrigerator in their liquor for up to 2 days. Drain before using.

Two-Bean Chili with Tofu and Cilantro

T his is an adaptation of a recipe for a vegetarian chili originally served at the La Costa Resort and Spa in Carlsbad, California, in the 1990s. It is served with brown rice and a pile of chopped tofu. As chilis go, it's a mild one, good for people who shy away from spicy foods. ● *Serves 8*

COOKER: Large round or oval
SETTING AND COOK TIME: LOW for 7 to 8 hours

2 medium-size onions, chopped

6 stalks celery, chopped

3 medium-size carrots or parsnips, peeled and chopped

1 large red bell pepper, seeded and finely chopped

1 large green bell pepper, seeded and finely chopped

2 cups peeled and cubed (1½-inch) butternut or acorn squash

1 medium-size sweet potato, peeled and diced

3 cups tomato juice

One 8-ounce can tomato sauce

Pinch of freshly ground white pepper

Pinch of cayenne pepper

1 to 2 tablespoons mild chili powder, to your taste

2 teaspoons ground cumin

1 teaspoon crumbled dried oregano

2 cups chopped ripe tomatoes

Two 16-ounce cans red kidney beans, undrained

Two 16-ounce cans chickpeas, undrained

TO SERVE:

12 to 16 corn tortillas

1 block firm or extra-firm tofu, drained and cut into ½-inch cubes

½ cup chopped fresh cilantro

2 limes, cut into wedges

1. In a very large skillet over medium-high heat, dry sauté the onions, celery, carrots, and bell peppers until their edges are browned; do this in batches if your pan is not extra-large. If your pan is hot enough, it will take a few minutes. Coat the inside of the crock with olive oil nonstick cooking spray and place the seared vegetables in the crock. Add the squash, sweet potato, tomato juice, tomato sauce, white pepper, cayenne, chili powder, cumin, oregano, chopped tomatoes, and beans to the crock; stir to combine. Cover and cook on LOW for 7 to 8 hours.

2. Wrap the tortillas in aluminum foil and warm in a preheated 300°F oven for 20 minutes (see Warming Tortillas, page 187, for other ways to warm the tortillas).

3. Serve the chili topped with some tofu and cilantro, with the warm tortillas and lime wedges on the side for squeezing into the chili.

Vegetarian 15-Bean Chili with Black Bean and Corn Salsa

I think I originally found this recipe on the Land O Lakes butter website, hence the butter in the chili, which is unusual. I had become enamored of the 15-bean combination packages and wanted to make something other than soup with them. This chili recipe can be easily doubled and frozen for future dinners. To freeze leftover chili in single servings, spoon 1⅓ cups chili into individual re-sealable plastic freezer containers or zipper-top plastic freezer bags. The chili can be frozen for up to 3 months. Thaw in the refrigerator for at least 24 hours, then reheat in the microwave or on the stovetop in a 2-quart saucepan over medium-low heat. ○ *Serves 6*

COOKER: Large round or oval
SETTINGS AND COOK TIMES: LOW for 8 to 10 hours, then HIGH for 20 minutes

One 8-ounce package dried 15-bean blend (discard spice packet)
2 tablespoons unsalted butter
2 medium-size carrots, chopped
1 large onion, chopped
1 clove garlic, minced
5 cups water
1 tablespoon chili powder
2 teaspoons ground cumin
1 teaspoon salt, or to taste
One 28-ounce can crushed tomatoes with roasted garlic
2 tablespoons tomato paste
Half of a 4-ounce can chopped jalapeño peppers, drained
2 tablespoons freshly squeezed lemon juice

BLACK BEAN AND CORN SALSA:

One 15-ounce can black beans, rinsed and drained

1 cup fresh, canned, or thawed frozen corn kernels

2 stalks celery, finely chopped

½ cup finely chopped red bell pepper

½ cup finely chopped green onions (white part and some of the green)

2 teaspoons finely minced jalapeño pepper

2 tablespoons chopped fresh cilantro

⅔ cup cider vinegar

⅓ cup light olive oil

Pinch of sugar

TO SERVE:

4 cups (1 pound) shredded Monterey Jack or cheddar cheese

1. Place the dried beans in the slow cooker and cover with cold water. Let soak overnight at room temperature. When ready to make the chili, drain.

2. Heat the butter in 10-inch skillet over medium-high heat until sizzling; add the carrots, onion, and garlic and cook, stirring a few times, until the onion is softened, about 5 minutes. Place the carrot mixture, 5 cups water, beans, chili powder, and cumin in the cooker and stir to combine. Cover and cook on LOW for 8 to 10 hours, until the beans are tender.

3. Combine the salsa ingredients in a medium-size bowl. Stir to coat all of the vegetables with the olive oil and vinegar. Let stand for 2 hours at room temperature, or cover and refrigerate until serving.

4. Increase the heat setting on the cooker to HIGH. Add the salt, tomatoes, tomato paste, jalapeños, and lemon juice. Cover and cook until heated through, about 20 minutes.

5. To serve, top each bowl of chili with plenty of cheese and a heaping ½ cup of salsa.

Turkey and Three-Bean Chili

I t's important to use ground dark turkey in this recipe; ground white turkey will dry out too fast. Add your favorite canned beans plus some mild chili beans (which are buttery and delicious) along with a can of refried beans, which contributes an appealing creamy texture to this chili. Of course, the real treat is serving it up with a variety of fresh, tasty toppings—your choice of olives, crumbled Mexican cheese, fresh tomatoes, and avocado slices. ○ *Serves 8*

COOKER: Large round or oval
SETTINGS AND COOK TIMES: HIGH for 2 hours, then LOW for 4 to 6 hours

2 tablespoons olive oil
1½ pounds ground dark turkey
1 medium-size onion, chopped
1 large green bell pepper, seeded and finely chopped
One 1.25-ounce package mild chili seasoning (I use McCormick's)
One 29-ounce can tomato sauce
Two 14.5-ounce cans diced tomatoes with sweet onions (I use Hunt's)
2 stalks celery, chopped
One 16-ounce can regular or vegetarian refried pinto beans
One 16-ounce can black beans, undrained
One 16-ounce can pinto beans, undrained
One 16-ounce mild chili beans (I use Bush's)

TO SERVE:
12 to 16 corn tortillas
8 ounces (2 cups) ranchero or feta cheese, crumbled
3 ripe Roma tomatoes, chopped
One 4-ounce can sliced black olives, drained
1 to 2 ripe avocados, peeled, pitted, and sliced

1. In a very large skillet over medium-high heat, heat the olive oil, then add the ground turkey and cook until the meat is browned, breaking it up into smaller pieces; drain or blot with paper towels to remove the fat. Transfer to the slow cooker.

2. Add the onion and green pepper to the skillet and cook, stirring a few times, until softened, about 5 minutes; add the chili seasoning and cook for 1 minute, then transfer to the cooker. Add the tomato sauce, diced tomatoes, celery, and beans to the cooker; stir to combine. Cover and cook on HIGH for 2 hours, then continue to cook on LOW for 4 to 6 hours.

3. Wrap the tortillas in aluminum foil and warm in a preheated 300°F oven for 20 minutes (see Warming Tortillas, below, for other ways to warm the tortillas). Serve the chili with the cheese, chopped tomatoes, sliced olives, and avocado slices on top and the warm tortillas on the side.

•• Warming Tortillas ••

If you don't have any cornbread or muffins to serve with your chili, then tortillas are the next best thing. You will want 1 to 3 corn tortillas per person, or 1 to 2 flour tortillas. Fresh tortillas, made the day you buy them, are best when eaten as a bread, but I also keep fresh flour tortillas in the freezer and reheat them quickly until soft and puffy in the toaster. Here are several different methods for warming tortillas.

In the oven: Preheat the oven to 400°F. Place individual corn or flour tortillas directly on the rack and bake until soft and pliable, 2 to 3 minutes. Or wrap a stack of 4 in aluminum foil or place the stack in a terra cotta tortilla warmer, and heat at 350°F for about 15 minutes.

On a cast-iron skillet or griddle: Heat an ungreased pan over medium-high heat until hot. Place a corn or flour tortilla on the surface and heat until just puffy, about 10 seconds. Turn once. If a crispy tortilla is desired, heat a tablespoon of oil in the pan before adding the tortilla.

On a stovetop grill or outdoor grill: Heat a gas grill or charcoal fire to medium-high heat. Place a corn or flour tortilla on the grill until just puffy, turning once.

In a microwave oven: Place corn or flour tortillas in a single layer on the microwave tray and warm until just puffy, about 30 seconds. Be careful, as tortillas overbaked in the microwave are very tough. Or wrap stacks of tortillas in waxed paper and microwave for 2-minute intervals until the stack is warm and pliable.

In a bamboo steamer: Wrap a stack of corn or flour tortillas in a clean dishtowel and place in a vegetable steamer basket over an inch of boiling water. Cover and steam until the stack is warm and pliable, 5 to 8 minutes.

Big Sky Bison Chili

Last Christmas, my sister Meg and her husband, Don, took the kids to Big Sky, Montana, for a family ski trip. Don had been there the year before with his ski buddies and recommended a great place for chili—The Cabin Bar & Grill, which is situated right next to the mountains. After tasting the house specialty, bison chili, Meg knew she had to have the recipe. The owners, Kelly and Curly Shea, kindly gave her the recipe; this is her adaptation for the slow cooker. Bison (or buffalo meat), which is lower in fat than beef and tastes remarkably like it, is very appealing to modern cooks: It is free-range, hormone-free, grass-fed meat. You can now find buffalo meat at many grocery stores, at farmers' markets, and online (www.localharvest.org). Because it is so low in fat, it needs to be braised or stewed at a low temperature for a long time in the slow cooker to keep it from drying out. Enjoy this chili with Honey-Top Cornbread (page 190). ● *Serves 6 to 8*

COOKER: Large round or oval
SETTING AND COOK TIME: LOW for 8 to 9 hours

2 tablespoons olive oil

1½ pounds ground bison or ground beef

1½ cups chopped onion

Two 14.5-ounce cans diced tomatoes with their juice

¼ cup chili powder

2 teaspoons ground cumin

1½ teaspoons ground coriander

¾ teaspoon crumbled dried sage

½ teaspoon ground allspice

Two 16-ounce cans black beans, rinsed and drained

One 16-ounce can pinto beans, rinsed and drained

2 cups water

½ cup low-sodium beef broth

2 canned chipotle chiles in adobo sauce, chopped

1 fresh green ancho chile, seeded, deveined, and chopped

Sour cream for serving

Shredded medium or sharp cheddar cheese for serving

Corn chips for serving

1. In a very large skillet over medium-high heat, heat 1 tablespoon of the olive oil, then add the ground bison and cook until the meat is browned, breaking it up into small pieces. Transfer the meat to the slow cooker. Add the remaining 1 tablespoon olive oil to the skillet, then add the onion and cook, stirring a few times, until softened, about 5 minutes; transfer the onion to the cooker. Add the tomatoes, chili powder, cumin, coriander, sage, allspice, beans, water, broth, chipotles, and ancho chile to the cooker; stir to combine. Cover and cook on LOW for 8 to 9 hours.

2. Serve the chili in bowls topped with dollops of sour cream, and with shredded cheese and corn chips on the side.

Slow Cooker Tip: Frozen Foods in the Slow Cooker

Never place frozen foods in the slow cooker unless a recipe specifically calls for it, as it delays the proper heating of the contents and lengthens the cook time. Never thaw foods of any type in the slow cooker.

•• Cornbread Hot from the Oven ••

Everyone seems to love cornbread. Here are two favorite recipes that are easy to mix and bake. Remember that cornbread is best served fresh from the oven.

Honey-Top Cornbread ○ Makes one 8- or 9-inch square cornbread

This cornbread is a bit sweet, very moist, and full of flavor. It is made extra delightful with a brushing of honey just as it comes out of the oven. Don't skip the vanilla; it adds so much to the taste. Bake in a pan or as individual breads in a muffin-top pan that creates muffins 4 inches in diameter and 1 inch deep. Serve with lots of butter.

1 cup fine-grind yellow cornmeal, preferably stone-ground
1 cup all-purpose flour or whole-wheat pastry flour
¼ cup sugar
1½ teaspoons baking powder
½ teaspoon baking soda
1 teaspoon salt
2 large eggs, slightly beaten
1 cup buttermilk
½ teaspoon pure vanilla extract
¼ cup (½ stick) unsalted butter, melted
2 tablespoons honey, for brushing

1. Preheat the oven to 350°F (325°F if using a Pyrex glass baking dish). Grease an 8- or 9-inch square ceramic or Pyrex baking dish. If using a ceramic baking dish, place it in the oven to heat up while mixing the batter.

2. Combine the cornmeal, flour, sugar, baking powder, baking soda, and salt in a large bowl. Make a well in the center of the dry mixture and add the eggs, buttermilk, vanilla, and melted butter. Stir with a whisk just until all the ingredients are moistened yet thoroughly blended. Take care not to overmix.

3. Pour the batter into the pan. Bake until golden around the edges and a cake tester inserted into the center comes out clean, 30 to 35 minutes. Cool on a wire rack.

4. Warm the honey in the microwave if it is too thick to brush. Brush the top of the hot cornbread with the honey and let it soak in. Let stand for 10 minutes, cut it into thick squares, and serve.

Corn Kernel Corn Muffins ● Makes 12 muffins

There is something just plain wonderful about fresh-out-of-the-oven corn muffins. These muffins are great to serve as an accompaniment to your chilis and stews, but they're also good with egg dishes and soups. Look for corn flour, the finest grind of cornmeal, in the specialty flour section of a well-stocked supermarket or natural foods store. I use Bob's Red Mill brand.

1 cup all-purpose flour
1 cup medium-grind yellow cornmeal, preferably stone-ground, or corn flour
⅓ cup sugar
2½ teaspoons baking powder
¼ teaspoon baking soda
½ teaspoon salt
1 cup buttermilk
½ cup frozen baby corn kernels, thawed, or kernels cut fresh off the cob
1 large egg
1 large egg yolk
3 tablespoons unsalted butter, melted
3 tablespoons light olive oil

1. Preheat the oven to 375°F. Butter or coat the wells of a 12-cup muffin tin with nonstick cooking spray, or use paper muffin liners.

2. In a medium-size bowl, combine the flour, cornmeal, sugar, baking powder, baking soda, and salt. Make a well in the center of the dry mixture and add the buttermilk, corn kernels, whole egg, egg yolk, melted butter, and olive oil. Stir just until all the ingredients are moistened yet thoroughly blended. Take care not to overmix. The batter will be thick and lumpy.

3. Spoon the batter into the muffin cups until almost level with the tops of the cups. Bake until the tops are golden, a cake tester comes out clean, and the tops of the muffins are springy to the touch, 20 to 25 minutes. Let stand for 5 minutes before turning the muffins out of the cups to cool on a wire rack. These are good to eat right away with butter but are also delicious at room temperature.

Creamy White Chicken Chili

This was dubbed the "The Best White Chili Ever" by my sister Meg, who loves anything and everything creamy. Serve with Corn Kernel Corn Muffins (page 191). • *Serves 8*

COOKER: Medium or large round or oval
SETTING AND COOK TIME: LOW for 4½ to 5½ hours; cilantro and chicken added in last hour; sour cream and half-and-half added in last 20 minutes

2 tablespoons unsalted butter
1 medium-size onion, chopped
Two 4-ounce cans diced roasted green chiles, drained
2 cups low-sodium chicken broth
Two 16-ounce cans white beans, like Great Northern, rinsed and drained
2 cloves garlic, pressed
2½ teaspoons crumbled dried oregano
1½ teaspoons ground cumin
½ teaspoon freshly ground white pepper
A couple of drops of Tabasco sauce, or to taste
Pinch of red pepper flakes
Leaves from 1 bunch fresh cilantro, chopped
1 rotisserie chicken, meat pulled off and bones and skin discarded
½ cup sour cream, plus more for serving
½ cup half-and-half
Shredded Monterey Jack cheese for serving

1. In a small skillet, heat the butter over medium-high heat until sizzling. Add the onion and cook, stirring a few times, until softened, about 5 minutes. Transfer the onion to the slow cooker. Add the green chiles, broth, beans, garlic, oregano, cumin, white pepper, Tabasco, and red pepper flakes. Cover and cook on LOW for 3 to 4 hours.

2. Add the cilantro and chicken meat to the cooker, cover, and continue to cook on LOW until the chicken is warm, about 1 hour. Before serving, stir in the sour cream and half-and-half until blended and cook until heated through, another 20 minutes.

3. Serve topped with shredded cheese and a dollop of sour cream.

Crock-Baked Potato and Chili Bar

One of the most fun ways to use the slow cooker is for making a pile of baked potatoes to be part of a potato bar, where you have lots of choices of delicious toppings and you can pile on any combination you like. This makes for a filling meal, whether you're serving just the family or a house full of people. ○ *Serves 8 to 12*

COOKER: Large round or oval
SETTING AND COOK TIME: HIGH for 3 to 4 hours, or LOW for 6 to 7 hours

12 large Idaho or russet potatoes
¼ cup olive oil
Fine sea salt

POTATO BAR CHOICES (MIX AND MATCH AS DESIRED):
1 recipe chili of your choice (pages 182 through 192)
1 to 2 cups salsa of your choice
1 cup ranch dressing
One 16-ounce container sour cream or sour cream substitute
3 cups (12 ounces) shredded mild or sharp Cheddar cheese
1 cup (4 ounces) freshly grated Parmesan cheese or crumbled soft goat cheese
Strips of smoked salmon or shredded rotisserie chicken
1 cup (2 sticks) unsalted butter, at room temperature, in a bowl or small crock
1 cup chopped fresh chives or green onions
½ cup chopped fresh Italian parsley or cilantro
8 slices bacon, cooked until crisp and crumbled
Oven-Roasted Barbecue Shrimp (page 194)
1 pound white or brown mushrooms, sliced and sautéed in 2 tablespoons butter until softened
1 cup sliced or chopped black olives
½ cup chopped smoked almonds
Paprika for sprinkling
Fleur de sel and a pepper grinder filled with black or multicolored peppercorns

1. Prick each potato with a fork or the tip of a sharp knife and rub with the olive oil. Sprinkle with salt and wrap each potato in a square of aluminum foil. Pile the potatoes into the slow cooker; do not add water. Cover and cook on HIGH for 3 to 4 hours or LOW for 6 to 7 hours (pierce with the tip of a knife to check for done-

ness). The more potatoes you have in the cooker, the longer the cook time will be. The potatoes will stay hot for hours on KEEP WARM.

2. When ready to serve, place the slow cooker on the table and surround it with bowls of your chosen toppings. Remove the potatoes from the cooker with tongs, and serve split open and piping hot, ready for the toppings. Eat immediately.

Oven-Roasted Barbecue Shrimp

You can also use these scrumptious shrimp as a topping for chili, along with sour cream and cilantro. ○ *Makes enough to top 8 to 10 potatoes*

6 tablespoons (¾ stick) unsalted butter
¼ cup olive oil
2 cloves garlic, minced
1 teaspoon freshly ground black pepper
1 tablespoon Worcestershire sauce
¼ teaspoon crumbled dried thyme
2 teaspoons hot pepper sauce
1½ pounds medium-size shrimp (23/30 count), peeled and deveined
Salt to taste

1. Preheat the oven to 375°F. Place a 9 x 13-inch metal baking pan or large cast-iron skillet in the oven for 10 minutes to heat up.

2. Once the pan is hot, add the butter, olive oil, garlic, pepper, Worcestershire sauce, thyme, and hot sauce. Stir to cook the garlic slightly. Add the shrimp and toss in the sauce to coat; even it out into one layer. Sprinkle with salt.

3. Place the pan in the oven and bake just until the shrimp are pink and firm, about 5 minutes. Stir once. Remove from the pan immediately and serve.

Crocked Sides and Veggie Main Courses

It used to be that casseroles were food for the winter months, too hot to make during the dog days of summer. But with the slow cooker, you won't heat up the kitchen, so casseroles are now a year-round choice for any meal. Finally, you can take advantage of fresh in-season fruits and vegetables—imagine eggplant Parmesan prepared with eggplant just out of the garden! But no matter the season, you'll find delicious side-dish and main-course vegetable creations in this chapter, including

slow cooker "baked" beans—perfect served alongside your favorite grilled dishes or paired with a second slow cooker full of ribs.

One of the most surprising foods to prepare in the slow cooker is bread stuffing. It comes out perfect, as moist as if it was cooked in the bird itself. So next holiday time, while the turkey fills the oven, let the stuffing cook to perfection on the counter in the slow cooker.

Chile Relleno Casserole

Relleno is the Spanish word for stuffed. This traditional Mexican dish is prepared by stuffing cheese into roasted whole chiles, then coating and frying them, a pretty time-consuming preparation. Then some inventive cook thought to layer the ingredients instead, and it's become one of the most popular casseroles in Mexican cooking. This is a lovely brunch or supper dish, served with a stack of hot tortillas and a crisp green salad. For a more substantial meal, offer it with beans and Mexican red rice. **o** *Serves 6*

COOKER: Large oval
SETTING AND COOK TIME: LOW for 4 to 5 hours

Two 7-ounce cans roasted whole green chiles, drained and rinsed, or 8 large fresh poblano
    chiles, stems, seeds, and membranes removed
2 cups (8 ounces) shredded cheddar cheese
2 cups (8 ounces) shredded Monterey Jack cheese
8 large eggs, beaten
1 cup all-purpose flour
1 teaspoon salt
1½ cups heavy cream
Warm salsa for serving
¾ cup low-fat sour cream, for serving

1. Coat the inside of the crock with nonstick cooking spray. Cut the chiles into 1-inch-thick strips. Place one-third of the chile strips in the bottom of the crock and top with one-third of the cheddar and one-third of the Jack cheese. Make a second layer of the chile strips, cheddar, and Jack cheese, then a third layer.

2. In a blender or food processor, or in a medium-size bowl with a whisk or immersion blender, combine the eggs, flour, salt, and cream, mixing until smooth. Pour the egg mixture into the cooker. Cover and cook on LOW for 4 to 5 hours, until the casserole is firm and the eggs are set. Take care not to let the casserole burn around the edges.

3. Serve hot, right from the crock, with the warm salsa and sour cream on the side.

Eggplant Parmesan

Eggplant is a member of the nightshade family and is close kin to the tomato and potato. While most people think of it as a vegetable, botanically speaking, it's really a great big plump berry. Use fresh eggplants within two days of purchase, as they get bitter if they sit longer. Young eggplants can be used unpeeled, but if you have a larger, fully mature one, go ahead and peel it. Eggplant Parmesan is one of the eggplant's finest moments. I have seen recipes that layer the eggplant raw, but giving the eggplant slices a crumb coating and roasting them first makes for a really special-tasting final dish. Definitely make this in an oval cooker.

○ *Serves 8*

COOKER: Large oval
SETTING AND COOK TIME: LOW for 4 to 5 hours

2 to 3 large eggplants (2 to 2½ pounds)
Salt to taste
One 28- or 32-ounce can whole tomatoes with their juice
1 clove garlic, cut in half
⅓ cup olive oil
Freshly ground black pepper to taste
3 large egg whites
3 tablespoons water
1 to 1½ cups fine dry bread crumbs
1 cup (4 ounces) freshly grated Parmesan cheese
1 pound fresh mozzarella cheese, sliced into ¼-inch-thick rounds
¼ cup slivered fresh basil leaves

1. Cut the stem and very bottom off each eggplant, then slice each crosswise into ½-inch-thick rounds. Arrange one layer in the bottom of a large colander set in a bowl or over the sink and sprinkle evenly and generously with salt. Repeat with the remaining eggplant slices, salting each layer, until all of the eggplant is piled in the colander. Weight down the slices with a couple of plates and let drain for 30 minutes to 1 hour. This will remove the bitterness and excess liquid. Press each eggplant slice with a paper towel to pat dry and wipe off any salt.

2. While the eggplant is draining, prepare the tomato sauce. Combine the tomatoes, garlic, and olive oil in a food processor and process until smooth. Season with salt and pepper and set aside.

3. Preheat the oven to 350°F. Coat two baking sheets and the inside of the crock with nonstick cooking spray.

4. Whisk the egg whites and water together in a shallow dish until frothy. Combine the bread crumbs and ¼ cup of the Parmesan in another shallow dish. Dip the eggplant slices into the egg-white mixture, then coat evenly with the bread crumb mixture. (Discard any leftover bread crumbs and egg whites.) Arrange the eggplant slices in a single layer on the prepared baking sheets. Bake for 15 minutes, then turn the eggplant slices over and bake until crisp and golden, about 15 minutes longer.

5. Spread about ½ cup of the tomato sauce over the bottom of the crock. Arrange one-third of the eggplant slices over the sauce, overlapping them slightly. Top with half of the mozzarella slices. Sprinkle with one-third of the Parmesan and half of the basil. Make a second layer of eggplant with half the remaining eggplant slices and top it with 1 cup of tomato sauce, the remaining mozzarella slices, half the remaining Parmesan, and the remaining basil. Make a last layer of eggplant slices, topped with the remaining tomato sauce and Parmesan. You will have three layers of eggplant.

6. Cover and cook on LOW for 4 to 5 hours, until bubbly and browned around the edges. Serve portioned out of the crock.

Lazy Day Cabbage Rolls

T he slow cooker is perfect for making cabbage rolls, but who has the time to assemble each individual roll? My friend Valerie Adams has the answer: Layer the cabbage and the "filling" and cook it as a casserole. You can prepare a vegetarian version of this by replacing the ground meat with vegetarian ground round (look for the Yves brand), a satisfying substitute for ground beef or turkey. If you make the veggie version, there's no need to brown the veggie ground round— just crumble it. The freshly prepared chunky salsa makes this dish really shine. You'll have a goodly amount left over, so enjoy it with chips. ○ *Serves 6*

COOKER: Large round or oval
SETTINGS AND COOK TIMES: LOW for 6 to 7 hours

2 pounds ground dark turkey or ground beef chuck
1 large head green cabbage (about 2 pounds)
2 tablespoons olive oil
One 16-ounce container small-curd cottage cheese or ricotta cheese
2 cups Valerie's Chunky Bell Pepper Salsa (recipe follows) or
    chunky fresh tomato salsa of your choice
2 cups raw converted rice
1 tablespoon minced fresh basil or ½ to 1 teaspoon dried basil
1 tablespoon minced fresh oregano or ½ to 1 teaspoon dried oregano
2 cups tomato juice
One 8-ounce container sour cream, for serving

1. In a large skillet over medium-high heat, brown the meat until no pink remains, 5 to 8 minutes, breaking it up into small pieces; set aside to cool until warm.

2. Core the cabbage and remove the outer layer of leaves. Chop the cabbage.

3. Coat the inside of the crock with nonstick cooking spray and pour the olive oil in the bottom.

4. In a medium-size bowl, combine the cooked beef, cottage cheese, salsa, rice, basil, and oregano until evenly blended.

5. Spread one-quarter of the chopped cabbage in the bottom of the crock. Spread one-third of the beef mixture over the cabbage. Repeat the layering two more times, then end with a layer of cabbage. Pour the tomato juice over the contents of the crock. Cover and cook on LOW for 6 to 7 hours, until the rice is fluffy and the cabbage is tender.

6. Serve hot, topped with dollops of sour cream.

Valerie's Chunky Bell Pepper Salsa

Makes 5 cups

1 red bell pepper, seeded and diced
1 green bell pepper, seeded and diced
Leaves from 1 bunch fresh cilantro, chopped
One 28-ounce can plum tomatoes, drained
3 tablespoons balsamic vinegar
1 teaspoon ground cumin

Combine all of the ingredients in a food processor; pulse a few times to combine and create a chunky mixture. Pour the salsa into a container, cover, and refrigerate for 4 hours to meld the flavors. The salsa will keep, refrigerated, for 1 week.

Winter Squash Stuffed with Sausage, Mushrooms, and Cranberries

T he appearance of freshly harvested winter squash is a sure sign of the approaching fall holiday season. I think steaming is the best way to cook winter squash, and the slow cooker does it wonderfully. All kinds of stuffing work well with winter squash since they make a natural bowl-like container for it. For this recipe, you will want to use a round squash with bright orange flesh, such as acorn, kabocha, golden nugget, or red kuri. This dish can stand on its own as a main dish, or be a side dish to turkey or other poultry. The skins of winter squash are really tough, so use a sturdy chef's knife when you cut into them. **o** *Serves 4*

COOKER: Large round or oval
SETTING AND COOK TIME: LOW for 6 to 7 hours

1 cup hot water
1 cup dried cranberries
⅔ cup hot apple juice
1 pound mild Italian sausage or fresh chicken apple sausage, casings removed
6 tablespoons (¾ stick) unsalted butter
½ cup chopped onion
8 ounces brown or white mushrooms, stemmed and chopped
1½ teaspoons crumbled dried sage
2 cups fresh whole-wheat bread crumbs (ground in a food processor)
Salt and freshly ground black pepper to taste
About ¼ cup low-sodium chicken broth or hot apple juice, for moistening
Two 1½- to 1 ¾-pound acorn squash

1. Coat the inside of the crock with olive oil nonstick cooking spray. Add the hot water to the crock.

2. In a small bowl, combine the cranberries and hot apple juice; let stand at room temperature.

3. In a large skillet over medium-high heat, cook the sausage until no longer pink, 4 to 5 minutes, breaking it up into small pieces; remove from the pan and set aside on a plate. Wipe out the skillet with paper towel, then melt the butter over medium-high heat until it sizzles, and add the onion, mushrooms, and sage. Cook, stirring occasionally, until the onion is softened and the mushrooms are cooked, about 5 minutes. Add the bread crumbs and stir until the crumbs brown lightly, about 3 minutes. Stir in the cranberries with their soaking liquid and the sausage; mix well. Season with salt and pepper. The mixture should be moist but not sticky and able to be clumped into a ball. If the mixture is too dry, add a little broth or more hot apple juice.

4. Halve the 2 squash through their "equators" and scoop out the seeds and stringy fibers; discard. Cut a thick piece off the bottoms of each so the halves will sit flat in the crock, being careful not to make a hole in the squash. Use an oversize spoon or your hands to fill each squash half with one-quarter of the stuffing mixture; pack lightly and fill until slightly mounded. Arrange the squash halves in a single layer in the crock. Cover and cook on LOW for 6 to 7 hours, until the squash are tender when pierced with the tip of a knife.

5. Remove the squash carefully with tongs and serve hot.

Spinach and Cheese Soufflé

This fantastic spinach dish is rich with cheeses and can be either a perfect side dish for simple roasted meats and poultry or stand on its own as a vegetarian main dish. The recipe is adapted from one in an early Rival slow cooker cookbook published in the 1960s. It is really easy to make—just put everything into the crock, stir, and let it cook. You can easily double or triple the recipe for parties, but be sure to use a large slow cooker. ○ *Serves 6 to 8*

COOKER: Medium round or oval
SETTING AND COOK TIME: LOW for 4 to 5 hours

Two 10-ounce packages frozen chopped spinach, thawed and squeezed dry
¼ cup (½ stick) unsalted butter, melted
2 cups (8 ounces) cubed cheddar cheese
2 cups (8 ounces) cubed Monterey Jack cheese
One 16-ounce container small-curd cottage cheese
Pinch of salt
3 large eggs, well beaten
¼ cup all-purpose or whole-wheat pastry flour

1. Coat the inside of the crock with olive oil nonstick cooking spray. Place all of the ingredients except the flour in the crock, sprinkling the flour over everything last and stirring with a wooden spoon to evenly combine everything.

2. Cover and cook on LOW for 4 to 5 hours, until the custard is set and a bit brown around the edges. Turn off the cooker and let the soufflé rest, covered, for 15 minutes before serving hot.

Lynn's Green Enchilada Casserole

This is from the kitchen of my friend Lynn Alley, who devised it when we were creating recipes for *Prevention* magazine. Think of it as free-form enchiladas—instead of rolling the filling in tortillas, the tortillas and filling are layered in the slow cooker, then topped with the sauce and cheese. Look for green chile enchilada sauce in the ethnic foods section of the supermarket; it is made with tomatillos instead of tomatoes. ○ *Serves 4*

COOKER: Large round or oval
SETTING AND COOK TIME: LOW for 3 to 4 hours

9 corn tortillas
1 medium-size butternut squash, peeled, seeded, and cut into 1-inch cubes
One 4.5-ounce can chopped black olives, drained
¼ cup chopped fresh cilantro
8 ounces baby spinach, coarsely chopped
One 19-ounce can mild green chile enchilada sauce (such as La Victoria brand)
2 cups (8 ounces) shredded mild cheddar, smoked Gouda, or Monterey Jack cheese

1. Coat the inside of the crock with nonstick cooking spray. Cover the bottom of the crock with 2 to 3 of the tortillas, overlapping them slightly.

2. In a large bowl, using your hands, toss together the squash, olives, cilantro, and spinach. Arrange half of this mixture over the tortillas in the crock, then top with 1 cup of the enchilada sauce and ½ cup of the cheese; repeat with the remaining squash mixture, and another layer of tortillas, sauce, and ½ cup cheese. Finish with a layer of tortillas and pour the remaining sauce over all. Cover and cook on LOW for 3 to 4 hours. Check the casserole at 3 hours by piercing it with a fork; the vegetables should be tender but not mushy.

3. Sprinkle the remaining 1 cup cheese over the casserole about 30 minutes before serving; replace the cover of the slow cooker. Serve directly out of the crock.

Stuffed Bell Peppers

Karin Schlanger and David Winsberg own Happy Quail Farms, a farm that grows a variety of peppers in the midst of urban East Palo Alto, California, and this recipe is one of their favorites. David grows a rainbow of bell peppers and a few hot peppers as well. For the most beautiful presentation of stuffed peppers, Karin suggests buying a variety of colors: red, yellow, orange, and chocolate (a deep purple-brown), as well as green. For individual servings, look for peppers that are squarish in shape and medium-size. David and Karin make the sauce with flavorful, fresh tomatoes as long as the season lasts, but it's fine to use canned tomatoes, too. Be sure to cook your grains first (or use leftovers). ◦ *Serves 6*

COOKER: Large round or oval
SETTING AND COOK TIME: LOW for 5 to 6 hours, or HIGH for 2½ to 3 hours

6 large bell peppers, in a variety of colors, tops cut off and reserved, seeds and
    membranes removed
2 tablespoons olive oil
2 medium-size onions, chopped
4 cups seeded and chopped ripe tomatoes or one 28- to 29-ounce can plum tomatoes,
    chopped and juices reserved
2 tablespoons minced fresh mint or 2 teaspoons dried mint
Salt and freshly ground black pepper to taste
1 pound ground dark turkey or lean ground beef
1½ cups cooked converted long-grain rice, brown rice, or Israeli couscous
2 tablespoons minced fresh Italian parsley

1. Coat the inside of the crock with olive oil nonstick cooking spray. Remove the stems from the tops of the bell peppers and discard the stems, then chop the tops. Set aside.

2. In a large skillet, heat the olive oil over medium-high heat. Add half of the onions and cook, stirring a few times, until softened, about 5 minutes. Add the tomatoes and their juice, and bring the sauce to a boil. Cook, stirring occasionally, until some of the liquid has evaporated and the sauce has thickened somewhat, 5 to 7 minutes. Stir in half of the mint. Taste the sauce and season with salt and pepper. Pour the sauce into the crock.

3. Place the ground meat, chopped peppers, and the remaining onion in the skillet (no need to wash it—it will still be hot) and cook over medium heat, breaking the meat up with a spatula as it cooks, until the meat is cooked through and the onion has begun to soften, 5 to 7 minutes. Remove the skillet from the heat, drain the meat or blot with paper towels to remove any excess fat, and stir in the cooked rice, the remaining mint, and the parsley. Add ¾ teaspoon salt and ⅛ teaspoon pepper, or to taste, and stir to combine. Use a spoon to fill each pepper with some of the meat mixture, packed lightly up to the top of the pepper. Arrange the peppers upright, side by side, in the crock. Do not stack; the peppers must be in a single layer.

4. Cover and cook on LOW for 5 to 6 hours or HIGH for 2½ to 3 hours. When ready, the peppers will be tender but still hold their shape. Serve the peppers with some of the tomato sauce spooned over or alongside them.

Twice-Crocked Stuffed Potatoes with Artichokes and Parmesan

For a side to go with your best pot roast or meatloaf, serve these stuffed potatoes nice and hot. It is best to use an oval cooker for stuffed potatoes, as it will hold them in a single layer. ○ *Serves 6*

COOKER: Large oval
SETTINGS AND COOK TIMES: HIGH for 4 to 6 hours, or LOW for 6 to 8 hours; then HIGH for 1 hour

6 large Idaho or russet potatoes
4 to 6 tablespoons unsalted butter, softened
One 8-ounce container sour cream
About ¼ cup milk, or as needed
¾ cup freshly grated Parmesan cheese, plus more for sprinkling
One 13- to 14-ounce can quartered artichoke hearts, drained and coarsely chopped
⅓ cup chopped green onions (white part and some of the green)
Salt to taste

1. Scrub each potato under cold running water, then prick the still dripping-wet potatoes with a fork or the tip of a sharp knife and pile them into the slow cooker; do not add water. Cover and cook on HIGH for 3 to 5 hours or LOW for 6 to 8 hours (pierce with the tip of a knife to check for doneness).

2. Remove the potatoes from the cooker with tongs and cut each in half lengthwise. Scoop out the center of each potato half with a large spoon, leaving ½ inch of potato all the way around to keep the shell intact; set the potato shells aside. Place the potato flesh in a bowl and add the butter, sour cream, and milk; mash with a fork until smooth. You want the mixture to be quite thick. Add the ¾ cup Parmesan, the artichokes, and the green onions. Season with salt. Spoon the filling back into the potato shells, mounding each. Set the stuffed potatoes in the crock in a single layer touching each other, and sprinkle with more Parmesan. Cover and cook on HIGH for 1 hour.

3. Remove the stuffed potatoes carefully from the cooker with tongs and serve immediately.

Vegetarian Chili and Cheese Casserole

T his is a unique chili recipe, adapted from one developed in a cooking class for the blind. Handed down fingertip to fingertip, says the recipe, this is exceptionally tasty, as well as easy to assemble and prepare. You layer the sauce with cheese and tortilla chips, and it cooks down to something in between a cornmeal soufflé and a Mexican lasagna. All it needs to make a meal is a green salad on the side. If doubling or tripling this recipe, use a large slow cooker. ○ *Serves 6*

COOKER: Medium or large round or oval
SETTING AND COOK TIME: HIGH for 2 to 2½ hours

1½ tablespoons olive oil
1 small yellow onion, finely chopped
One 28-ounce can diced tomatoes, drained
One 4-ounce can diced roasted green chiles, drained
One 1-ounce package taco seasoning (I use McCormick's) or 2 tablespoons taco seasoning
7 to 8 ounces (about half of a 13.5-ounce bag) tortilla chips
4 cups (1 pound) shredded Colby and Monterey Jack cheese blend
1 cup sour cream

1. In a deep, medium-size saucepan, warm the olive oil, then cook the onion, stirring a few times, until softened, about 5 minutes. Add the tomatoes, chiles, and taco seasoning; stir to combine. Simmer, covered, for 20 to 30 minutes. The sauce can be made up to 2 days ahead and refrigerated.

2. Coat the inside of the crock with nonstick cooking spray. Arrange a layer of tortilla chips over the bottom of the crock, then spoon on one-third of the sauce and sprinkle with one-third of the cheese. Repeat the layers two more times, then use a rubber spatula or the back of a spoon to spread the sour cream on top. Cover and cook on HIGH for 2 to 2½ hours, until hot and browned around the edges. Serve spooned out of the crock.

Best Western One-Pot Beans

My sister Meg's family went to a going-away barbecue several years ago for her husband's former boss. There was a lot of delicious buffet-style food, including these sweet and savory baked beans. Meg got the recipe and has reworked it here using turkey bacon instead of pork, but you can use regular bacon if you like. Serve these beans with garlic bread and a green salad for an old-fashioned one-pot meal that's so tasty even the kids will ask for seconds. ● *Serves 8*

COOKER: Large round or oval
SETTING AND COOK TIME: LOW for 7 to 8 hours

8 ounces lean ground beef
10 slices turkey bacon, chopped
½ large yellow onion, finely chopped
One 15-ounce can pork and beans
One 16-ounce can red kidney beans, rinsed and drained
One 15.5-ounce can butter beans, rinsed and drained
½ cup firmly packed brown sugar
2 tablespoons granulated sugar
½ cup ketchup
¼ cup barbecue sauce of your choice, store-bought or homemade (page 118)
2 tablespoons light molasses (not blackstrap)
2 tablespoons Dijon mustard
½ teaspoon salt
½ teaspoon freshly ground black pepper
½ teaspoon chili powder

1. In a medium-size skillet, cook the ground beef and bacon together over medium-high heat until browned, breaking up the beef into small pieces; drain off the fat and place the mixture in the slow cooker. In the same skillet, cook the onion, stirring a few times, until softened, about 5 minutes. Add the onions and all of the beans to the cooker.

2. In a medium-size bowl, combine the sugars, ketchup, barbecue sauce, molasses, mustard, salt, pepper, and chili powder. Pour the mixture into the cooker and stir gently to coat the beans evenly. Cover and cook on LOW for 7 to 8 hours, until hot and bubbly. Serve spooned out of the crock.

Molasses and Brown Sugar Baked Beans

T his recipe makes a big ol' pot of beans—perfect for large parties. It is adapted from a recipe from Ernie Raffo Motter of Petaluma, California, who makes them all the time in the summer. It is dramatically simple and quick to assemble from ingredients right out of the pantry. I like the combination of half light and half dark brown sugar, but you can use all of one or the other. The beans can also conveniently cook overnight. People love 'em. ● *Serves 10 to 20*

COOKER: Medium round or oval
SETTING AND COOK TIME: LOW for 9 to 11 hours

4 strips lean smoky bacon, cut into thirds
Six 16-ounce cans pork and beans
1 cup light molasses (not blackstrap)
½ cup firmly packed light brown sugar
½ cup firmly packed dark brown sugar

1. In a medium-size skillet over medium heat, cook the bacon until it's just beginning to brown, but still soft. Drain on paper towels.

2. Combine the beans, molasses, and brown sugars in the slow cooker and stir well. Lay the cooked bacon over the top, pressing the pieces into the beans. Cover and cook on LOW for 9 to 11 hours. You can leave the beans for up to 2 hours on the KEEP WARM setting before serving.

Meg's Sage and Mushroom Country Bread Stuffing

My sister Meg has been making stuffing with fresh bread for years. She came up with this version since she likes her stuffing very moist, as if it had been cooking in the turkey for hours. She originally had prepared it in the oven, but after my book *Not Your Mother's Slow Cooker Cookbook* (The Harvard Common Press, 2005) was published, Meg switched to cooking it in the slow cooker. Not only does it stay nice and moist, it leaves room in the oven for cooking the rest of the meal. ○ *Serves 10*

COOKER: Large round or oval
SETTINGS AND COOK TIMES: HIGH for 1 hour, then LOW for 4 to 5 hours

½ cup olive oil
¼ cup (½ stick) unsalted butter
2 medium-size onions, chopped
4 stalks celery with leaves, diced
8 ounces white mushrooms, sliced
1 teaspoon salt
1 teaspoon freshly ground black pepper
Leaves from 1 bunch fresh Italian parsley
1½ teaspoons crumbled dried sage
1 teaspoon crumbled dried thyme
Two 1-pound loaves country French bread, with crusts left on, cut into big chunks
3 cups low-sodium chicken broth
3 large eggs
3 tablespoons chopped fresh sage

1. Heat the oil and butter together in a large skillet over medium heat until the butter sizzles, then add the onions and celery; cook, stirring a few times, until softened, about 5 minutes. Add the mushrooms and cook until their liquid has evaporated, 3 to 4 minutes. Add the salt, pepper, parsley, dried sage, and thyme and mix well.

2. Coat the inside of the crock with nonstick cooking spray. Add the bread pieces. In a large measuring cup, beat the broth and eggs together. Add the sautéed vegetables and the broth mixture to the crock. Mix with a rubber spatula until the ingredients are well combined and the bread is evenly moistened. Cover and cook on HIGH for 1 hour.

3. Open the lid and stir in the fresh sage. Set the cooker to LOW, cover, and cook for 4 to 5 hours, until the stuffing is puffy and nicely browned around the edges. The stuffing can sit in the cooker, covered, on KEEP WARM for up to 1 hour before serving. Serve hot right out of the crock.

Cornbread and Challah Bread Stuffing

For this recipe you need to make the cornbread, using white cornmeal, a few days before, so you can use it dried out in the stuffing. Add the broth to the stuffing a little at a time, mixing with a wooden spoon, until it is nice and moist to get the best texture in the finished stuffing. Be sure to use the challah bread; it adds a particular sweetness and texture. ● *Serves 6*

COOKER: Medium round or oval
SETTINGS AND COOK TIMES: HIGH for 1 hour, then LOW for 4 to 5 hours

1 cup white cornmeal
1 cup all-purpose flour
2 tablespoons sugar
1 tablespoon baking powder
½ teaspoon salt
2 large eggs
1 cup buttermilk
¼ cup light olive oil

¼ cup (½ stick) unsalted butter
2 large yellow onions, diced
4 stalks celery, chopped
Six to eight 1-inch-thick slices challah egg bread, toasted and torn or chopped
1 large egg (optional), beaten
Two 14.5-ounce cans low-sodium chicken broth, heated to boiling
2 to 3 teaspoons poultry seasoning
Salt to taste
A few grinds of black or white pepper
2 tablespoons unsalted butter, cut into pieces, for dotting top

1. Prepare the cornbread 2 to 3 days ahead of making the stuffing. Preheat the oven to 375°F. Combine the cornmeal, flour, sugar, baking powder, and salt in a large bowl. In a medium-size bowl, whisk together the eggs, buttermilk, and olive oil. Add to the dry ingredients and stir just until all the ingredients are moistened yet thoroughly blended. Take care not to overmix. Pour the batter into a greased 8-inch square or round springform pan. Bake until golden around the edges and a cake tester inserted into the center comes out clean, 20 to 25 minutes. Let cool completely in the pan, then break up the cornbread and place in a bowl. Let the cornbread dry at room temperature until you're ready to make the stuffing.

2. To prepare the stuffing, heat the butter in a large skillet over medium heat until it sizzles, then add the onions and celery and cook, stirring a few times, until softened, about 5 minutes.

3. Coat the inside of the crock with nonstick cooking spray. Add the cornbread and challah pieces. If using the egg, in a large measuring cup, beat together the egg and ¼ cup of the broth. Add the onion mixture, poultry seasoning, salt, pepper, and egg mixture to the crock. Mix with a rubber spatula until well combined and the bread is evenly moistened. Add hot broth slowly until the desired consistency is reached. Dot with the butter and sprinkle with a few tablespoons more of broth. Cover and cook on HIGH for 1 hour, then set to LOW and cook for 4 to 5 hours, until the stuffing is puffy and nicely browned around the edges. The stuffing can sit in the cooker, covered, on KEEP WARM for up to 2 hours before serving. Serve hot right out of the crock.

•• Tips for Tasty Slow Cooker Stuffings ••

○ A 1-pound loaf of bread will yield about 6 cups of cubed bread, a 1½-pound loaf will yield about 9 cups of cubed bread, and a 2-pound loaf will yield about 12 cups of cubed bread. White bread will give a lighter texture to your stuffing than whole wheat or whole grain. You can use anything from French bread to focaccia. Around the holidays, small bakeries will often bag their day-old bread, in delightful combinations, for use in stuffings; keep an eye out for them. If you use cornbread, make it the day before. You can also use packaged stuffing mix, if desired.

○ Never use raw meats or fish, especially pork products or oysters, in stuffings. Loose pork sausage or any type of raw sausage must be cooked completely, whether sautéed, baked, boiled, or grilled, before adding it to the stuffing mix.

○ If you are using really stale bread, you need to soak it in chicken broth or milk to soften it a bit. Fresh bread doesn't soak up the same amount of liquid. You can use fresh bread cubed and dried in the oven, day-old bread cut into cubes and air-dried overnight, or a package of seasoned commercial stuffing mix.

○ Adding leafy vegetables, such as Swiss chard or parsley, lightens the texture of a stuffing.

○ There is a guideline for the amount of liquid needed to moisten each recipe, but you can add more or less, depending on how moist or crumbly you like your stuffing.

○ Spoon the stuffing loosely into the crock, rather than packing it in, to allow room for the stuffing to expand as it heats up.

○ You will serve about ½ to 1 cup of prepared stuffing per person. Take into account your love of leftovers when deciding how much to make.

○ Transfer leftover stuffing to a covered storage container and refrigerate.

Pasta, Polenta, and Rice

I like to say that pasta, polenta, and risotto are the triumvirate of Italian comfort foods. A slow cooker book on family cooking wouldn't be complete without them.

Pasta is great family food. In this chapter, I offer you a nice selection of homemade sauces for the slow cooker, both with and without meat, as well as a range of Italian pasta casseroles. There are three recipes for lasagna, using dried, no-cooking-necessary pasta sheets, so you save time

by not precooking the noodles. I also offer recipes for mac and cheese, a chili macaroni made with turkey, jumbo stuffed shells, and a great ziti and sausage casserole that goes into the crock as fast as can be. Get some crunchy bread sticks or crusty Italian bread, toss a salad, and you will have a feast.

The slow cooker does a glorious job of making fluffy and delectable polenta, with no stirring involved. Polenta is a wonderful side dish with a braised beef stew or chicken cacciatore. Keep two slow cookers side by side so you can make your main dish in one and have the polenta sputtering away in another.

Polenta is a very coarse grind of cornmeal and takes a bit of time to soften and cook properly. You can use medium-grind yellow cornmeal (stone-ground has an especially nice flavor), which will cook faster.

There are lots of ways to serve polenta. The quickest is in a soft mound, sprinkled

with Parmesan cheese and topped with a pat of butter. You can also pour the hot polenta on a marble board or into a greased pan to cool; it will stiffen yet still be quite tender. Then you can cut it into slices and fry them in butter or olive oil to serve alongside roasted meats or egg dishes.

Like polenta, stovetop risotto normally requires a lot of stirring. The slow cooker liberates you from that. The only important technique to note is that the cook time must be strictly adhered to, as risotto can easily be overcooked. Risotto is traditionally eaten as a first course in Italy, served in a shallow bowl with a spoon and washed down with a nice wine, but I like it as a main dish. The vegetable versions are especially good for children.

Use short-grain Arborio rice for risotto. It is labeled *fino* or *supra fino*. Lesser grades are labeled *fino, semi-fino,* and *commune,* and are fine to use in soups. Lundberg Family Farms of California sells a domestic California Arborio that is giving

Italian Arborio some competition. Rice Select offers a Texas Arborio (called risotto rice), and CalRiso has another domestic version of Arborio that is a hybrid of Italian and California rice varieties; all are acceptable substitutes for Italian Arborio.

A 500-gram (just over 1 pound) bag of Arborio yields about 2 cups of raw rice.

But risotto isn't the only rice dish you can make in the slow cooker and I've included a selection of my favorites. Give them a try!

Slow Cooker Tip: Slow Cooker Settings and Temperatures

There are two cook settings on most slow cookers: LOW and HIGH. The LOW setting uses 80 to 185 watts and cooks in the temperature range of 170° to 200°F. The HIGH setting is double the wattage, 160 to 370 watts, and cooks at a temperature of 280° to 300°F, with slight variations due to the size of the cooker, the temperature of the food, and how full the crock is. There is also a KEEP WARM setting, but that is not to be used for cooking or reheating food. Every machine seems to cook a little bit differently, and only by using your machine will you learn how to gauge the cook time.

To check the temperature of your slow cooker, fill it three-quarters full with water, cover with the lid, and heat on LOW for 8 hours. Lift the lid and check the water temperature with an instant-read dial or digital thermometer. The temperature should register 185°F. If it is a bit higher, you will know to adjust your cook time slightly down, to prevent overcooking. If the temperature is lower, you may not be reaching the food-safe temperature of 140°F fast enough and should not use that cooker; exchange or discard it and buy a new one.

The Easiest Lasagna Bianco

You will love this recipe. After seeing a lasagna *bianco* recipe in *Gourmet* magazine, I immediately set out to adapt it for the slow cooker. The secrets are a jar of prepared Alfredo sauce and no-boil lasagna sheets, a new must-have in your pantry. In 3½ hours you will be serving a perfect lasagna—dripping with mozzarella cheese—right down to the rippled top layer and golden brown edges. In the slow cooker, the moisture from the sauce is plenty to cook the lasagna noodles perfectly every time. If you like, you can add two layers of vegetables to this lasagna, such as cooked fresh chard leaves, strips of roasted red peppers, leftover roasted mixed vegetables, thawed frozen or jarred water-packed artichoke hearts, sautéed mushrooms, or even a layer of pesto (but then it won't be a pure *bianco*); the total cook time will increase by about 30 minutes. ○ *Serves 4 to 6*

COOKER: Medium or large oval
SETTING AND COOK TIME: HIGH for 3½ to 4 hours

6 tablespoons olive oil
4 large shallots, chopped
One 16-ounce jar prepared Alfredo sauce
1 cup low-sodium chicken broth
3 tablespoons dry Marsala
1 cup (4 ounces) freshly grated Parmesan cheese
8 sheets no-cook oven-ready lasagna noodles
12 ounces whole-milk mozzarella cheese, thinly sliced or cubed

1. In a medium-size skillet, heat the oil over medium-low heat, then add the shallots and cook, stirring a few times, until they are soft and well cooked but not browned, about 8 minutes. Set aside to cool until warm.

2. In a medium-size bowl, combine the Alfredo sauce, broth, Marsala, cooked shallots, and ½ cup of the Parmesan.

3. Coat the inside of the crock with olive oil nonstick cooking spray. Using an over-size spoon, spread a big spoonful of the Alfredo mixture over the bottom of the crock. Break one pasta sheet into pieces and cover the Alfredo with the pieces; it doesn't matter what shape or size the pieces are, just break the sheet to fit. You will use about 2 sheets per layer. Cover the pasta with spoonfuls of sauce and one-quarter of the mozzarella. Add another layer of pasta pieces, Alfredo, and mozzarella; repeat 2 more times, then spread the top with any remaining Alfredo and sprinkle with the remaining ½ cup Parmesan.

4. Cover and cook on HIGH for 3½ to 4 hours. Test for tenderness by piercing the lasagna with the tip of a sharp knife at 3 to 3½ hours. The lasagna can be kept in the crock on the KEEP WARM setting for up to 1 hour before serving. Serve right out of the crock, cutting pieces with a plastic spatula.

Chicken and Roasted
Red Bell Pepper Lasagna

O ne of the best commercial convenience products to use in the slow cooker is jarred Alfredo sauce. While the sauce is quite bland on its own, it is remarkably stable in the slow cooker environment and is the perfect base for a variety of savory vegetable flavors. Here it is used in a sauce for a creamy chicken and vegetable lasagna. For the chicken, you can use Crock-Poached Chicken Breasts (page 58) or a store-bought rotisserie chicken. ● *Serves 10*

COOKER: Large oval
SETTING AND COOK TIME: HIGH for 4 to 5 hours

Two 12-ounce jars roasted red bell peppers, drained
Two 16-ounce jars prepared Alfredo sauce
½ cup freshly grated Parmesan cheese
½ teaspoon red pepper flakes
4 to 5 cups finely chopped cooked chicken
Three 8-ounce tubs chive and onion cream cheese (I use Philadelphia brand)
One 14- to 16-ounce bag frozen chopped spinach, thawed and squeezed dry
Salt and freshly ground black pepper to taste
One 9-ounce box no-cook oven-ready lasagna noodles (12 to 16 sheets)
2 medium-size zucchini, coarsely shredded
4 cups (1 pound) shredded Italian three-cheese blend

1. Puree the bell peppers, Alfredo sauce, Parmesan, and red pepper flakes in a food processor or in a large bowl using an immersion blender; set aside.

2. In another large bowl, combine the chicken, cream cheese, and spinach; season with salt and pepper.

3. To assemble the lasagna, coat the inside of the crock with olive oil nonstick cooking spray. Using a large spoon, spread 1 cup of the sauce over the bottom of the crock. Arrange sheets of pasta to cover the sauce; break the sheets into pieces to fit the curves of the crock (it doesn't matter what shape or size the pieces are, just that they fit). You will use about 3 sheets per layer. On top of the pasta, add one-quarter of the chicken-spinach mixture, a sprinkling of zucchini, and 1 cup of the three-cheese blend. Repeat the layers of pasta, chicken-spinach mixture, zucchini, and cheese, ending with the cheese, until all the ingredients are used. The lasagna will fill the crock a good three-quarters full; it will collapse as it cooks.

4. Cover and cook on HIGH for 4 to 5 hours. Test for tenderness by piercing the lasagna with the tip of a sharp knife at 3½ hours. The edges will be browned. The lasagna can be kept in the crock on the KEEP WARM setting for up to 1 hour before serving. Serve right out of the crock, portioning pieces with a plastic spatula.

Deep-Dish Spinach and Ricotta Pie

This is a favorite Neapolitan-style lasagna. Again, use the no-boil dried lasagna noodles. Homemade ricotta is ridiculously easy to make and mouthwatering in its delectability. Delicious! ● *Serves 8*

COOKER: Large oval
SETTING AND COOK TIME: HIGH for 4 to 5 hours

Two 25- to 26-ounce jars prepared marinara sauce
¼ cup homemade, thawed frozen, or prepared basil pesto
Two 15-ounce containers ricotta cheese (whole milk preferred) or
    2 recipes Homemade Ricotta (recipe follows)
2 large eggs, lightly beaten
One 14- to 16-ounce package frozen chopped spinach, thawed and squeezed dry
1¾ cups (7 ounces) freshly grated Parmesan cheese
One 9-ounce box no-cook oven-ready lasagna noodles (12 to 16 sheets)
1 pound mozzarella cheese, thinly sliced or cubed

1. Coat the inside of the crock with olive oil nonstick cooking spray. Place 1½ jars of the marinara in a bowl and swirl in the pesto. Using a large spoon, spread ½ cup of the sauce over the bottom of the crock.

2. In a medium-size bowl, combine the ricotta, eggs, spinach, and ¾ cup of the Parmesan until well mixed.

3. Break one pasta sheet into pieces and cover the bottom of the crock with the pieces; it doesn't matter what shape or size the pieces are, just break them to fit (you will use 2 to 3 sheets per layer); they will expand during cooking. Cover with ½ cup of sauce and one-third of the mozzarella. Add another layer of pasta, then ½ cup sauce and ¼ cup Parmesan. Add another layer of pasta (the third layer) and spread with half the ricotta mixture, then cover with ½ cup of sauce and ¼ cup Parmesan. Repeat again with the pasta, the remaining ricotta, ½ cup sauce, and ¼ cup Parmesan. Then layer in pasta, ½ cup sauce, and half the remaining mozzarella. Press down gently to compress a bit. Finish with 1 full cup of the plain marinara sauce (you might not use all of the sauce) and the remaining Parmesan and mozzarella. The lasagna will fill the crock two-thirds to three-quarters full; it will compress as it cooks.

4. Cover and cook on HIGH for 4 to 5 hours, until the top layer is rippled and golden brown around the edges. Test for tenderness by piercing the lasagna with the tip of a sharp knife at 3 hours. The lasagna can sit in the cooker on KEEP WARM for up to 2 hours before serving. Serve right out the crock, portioning pieces with a metal or plastic spatula.

Homemade Ricotta

Fluffy, fresh ricotta cheese can be made at home in about an hour. The recipe can be doubled. You can also use this as a topping on pasta and marinara instead of Parmesan cheese. ● *Makes 1 pound, about 2 cups*

8 cups organic whole milk
¾ cup heavy cream (organic or not ultra-pasteurized)
2 teaspoons salt
2 cups buttermilk
¼ cup distilled white vinegar

1. Line a colander with at least 4 layers of cheesecloth and place the colander in the sink.

2. Combine the milk, cream, and salt in a large saucepan. Over medium heat, heat until the mixture is steaming hot. When it reaches 175° to 180°F on a candy or meat thermometer, stir in the buttermilk and vinegar. Keep the heat at a consistent level.

3. When curds form on the surface and separate from the whey, gently ladle the curds with a skimmer or slotted spoon into the colander. (The whey looks like cloudy gray water underneath a mass of thick white curds.) Every 10 minutes, gently ladle the curds into the colander.

4. When all the curds are in the colander, let them drain for about 15 minutes. When the dripping has slowed, gently gather the edges of the cheesecloth and twist to bring the curds together; do not squeeze. Place in a container, remove the cheesecloth, cover tightly, and refrigerate until ready to use. Discard the whey. The ricotta will keep in the refrigerator for up to 1 week.

Baked Ziti with Sausage

This is loosely adapted from a recipe in Mark Bittman's cookbook *Mark Bittman's Quick and Easy Recipes from the New York Times* (Broadway Books, 2007), which is a collection of recipes from his column entitled "The Minimalist." This is a glorious casserole, one of the most beloved Italian pasta dishes, elegant in its rustic simplicity. The bits of creamy mozzarella are distributed throughout the pasta, giving delight in each bite. ○ *Serves 6*

COOKER: Medium or large round or oval
SETTING AND COOK TIME: LOW for 4 to 4½ hours

1 pound mild Italian sausage, casings removed
1 large onion, diced
2 cloves garlic, minced
One 28-ounce can Italian plum tomatoes with their juice, chopped
One 8-ounce can tomato sauce
Salt and freshly ground black pepper to taste
1 pound ziti, rigatoni, or other large-cut tube pasta
1 pound whole-milk mozzarella, cubed
½ cup freshly grated Parmesan cheese

1. Bring a large pot of salted water to boil for the pasta. Coat the inside of the crock with olive oil nonstick cooking spray.

2. In a large skillet over medium-high heat, cook the sausage until browned on one side, about 5 minutes, breaking it into small pieces. Stir, then cook for another 2 minutes. Add the onion and garlic; cook for a minute or two until just softened. Add the tomatoes and tomato sauce; bring to a boil. Reduce the heat to a simmer; season with salt and pepper.

3. Meanwhile, cook the pasta until just *al dente*; it should still be a bit too chewy to eat. Drain and pour the pasta into the crock. Add the tomato sauce, and stir in three-quarters of the mozzarella. Sprinkle with the remaining mozzarella and the Parmesan on top. Cover and cook on LOW for 4 to 4½ hours.

4. Serve hot from the crock with nice crusty bread.

Stuffed Shells with Mushroom Tomato Sauce

I have a weakness for shopping in the big warehouse stores, and I usually pick up a bag of giant stuffed shells from the freezer section. They are as good as I can make from scratch, with a nice thick stuffing of ricotta. Place them in the crock frozen, pour your favorite marinara sauce (or my doctored-up version here) over the shells, and leave it to cook all day on LOW. It doesn't get any easier than this, and it is pure comfort food, vegetarian-style. ○ *Serves 6*

COOKER: Large round or oval
SETTING AND COOK TIME: LOW for 8 hours

One 20-ounce bag frozen giant cheese-stuffed pasta shells
One 28- to 29-ounce jar prepared marinara sauce
¼ cup dry red wine
3 tablespoons tomato paste
8 ounces white mushrooms, sliced
2 tablespoons extra-virgin olive oil
½ cup freshly grated Parmesan cheese, for serving
Chopped fresh Italian parsley for serving

1. Coat the inside of the crock with olive oil nonstick cooking spray. Arrange the shells in the bottom of the crock; it's okay if they touch.

2. In a medium-size bowl, whisk together the marinara, wine, and tomato paste. Stir in the mushrooms and olive oil. Pour the mixture over the shells. Cover and cook on LOW for 8 hours, until the pasta is tender when pierced with the tip of a knife.

3. Serve the shells hot from the crock; sprinkle with the Parmesan and parsley. Serve with some crusty bread to sop up the sauce.

Shrimp Marinara

T omato sauce and plump shrimp (lots of shrimp in less than the usual amount of sauce) is a favorite alternative to a meat sauce. Be sure that you do not overcook the shrimp at the end, or they will be tough. Usually sauces with seafood do not include Parmesan cheese, but somehow I always need it because it just tastes so good. Serve this with a leafy green salad and crusty garlic bread. ○ *Serves 6*

COOKER: Large round or oval
SETTING AND COOK TIME: LOW for 5 to 6 hours, then HIGH for 15 minutes

One 28-ounce can plum tomatoes with their juice, chopped or crushed with your hands
Two 6-ounce cans tomato paste
½ cup dry white wine
2 cloves garlic, finely chopped
1 teaspoon crumbled dried oregano
1 teaspoon crumbled dried basil
Pinch of red pepper flakes
Salt and freshly ground black pepper to taste
2 pounds medium-size shrimp (23/30 count), peeled and deveined
1½ pounds linguine
1 cup (4 ounces) freshly grated Parmesan cheese, for serving

1. Coat the inside of the crock with olive oil nonstick cooking spray. Add the tomatoes, tomato paste, wine, garlic, oregano, basil, and red pepper flakes. Cover and cook on LOW for 5 to 6 hours.

2. Season the sauce with salt and pepper and set the cooker to HIGH. Add the shrimp, cover, and cook for 15 minutes, until the shrimp are pink and firm.

3. Meanwhile, cook the linguine according to the package directions. Drain and serve immediately, with the sauce ladled over the pasta and sprinkled with some Parmesan cheese.

Essential Marinara Sauce

Marinara sauce is a quick and easy all-purpose sauce. Every cook needs one in her culinary pocket for using over pasta or in casseroles. With this recipe, you can load the ingredients into the slow cooker and let it bubble away. If you want to make enough to freeze an extra portion, double this recipe; make sure to use a large cooker. If you can find it, get the Italian tomato paste that comes in tubes for convenience; it tastes brighter than the stuff sold in cans. This sauce is also nice made with canned golden tomatoes if you happen to find them on your supermarket shelf. You can flavor this sauce with herbs, Italian style, or the zest of an orange, Provence style, but not both at the same time. Since this is such a light sauce, serve it over angel hair pasta, gemelli twists, mostaccioli, shells, radiatore, or fusilli. ● *Makes about 5 cups*

COOKER: Medium or large round or oval
SETTING AND COOK TIME: LOW for 4 to 5 hours

5 tablespoons olive oil
2 large shallots, finely chopped
Two 28-ounce cans whole plum tomatoes with their juice
One 6-ounce can or tube tomato paste
¼ cup dry red wine or vodka
½ teaspoon crumbled dried mixed Italian herbs or grated zest of 1 large orange
Salt and freshly ground black pepper to taste
¼ cup (½ stick) unsalted butter or crème fraîche (optional)

1. In a medium-size skillet, warm the olive oil over medium heat, then add the shallots and cook, stirring, until softened, 3 to 4 minutes. Place the shallots and oil, tomatoes, tomato paste, wine, and herbs or orange zest in the slow cooker. Cover and cook on LOW for 4 to 5 hours.

2. Season the sauce with salt and pepper. Use an immersion blender to puree it. Swirl in the butter, for a little bit richer sauce, or the crème fraîche, for a creamy sauce, if using. If not serving the sauce with hot pasta immediately, you can hold it in the slow cooker on KEEP WARM for a few hours. The sauce will keep, in a tightly covered container, in the refrigerator for up to 3 days or in the freezer for up to 2 months.

Big-Batch Home-Style Meat Sauce

Sometimes a family has a favorite spaghetti sauce that lives on from genera-tion to generation; kids grow up and serve it to their kids. This is that kind of sauce. Simmer it all day in the slow cooker and ladle it over a sturdy dried pasta like spaghetti, bucatini, pappardelle, or ziti, or on cheese ravioli, with lots of real Parmigiano-Reggiano for sprinkling. This recipe calls for canned tomato sauce, which is nice and smooth; do not substitute any other canned tomato product. Use 4 to 6 cups of the finished sauce for 1 pound of pasta and have leftovers for another meal or for freezing. Serve with a leafy green salad and crusty garlic bread.

○ *Makes about 18 cups, enough for 3 pounds of pasta to serve 12 hungry pasta lovers*

COOKER: Large round or oval
SETTING AND COOK TIME: LOW for 8 to 9 hours;
   herbs added halfway through cooking time

½ cup olive oil
2 medium-size yellow onions, chopped
2 cloves garlic, finely chopped
2 pounds lean ground beef chuck or ground dark turkey
Salt and freshly ground black pepper to taste
Five 29-ounce cans tomato sauce (I use Hunt's)
1 tablespoon crumbled dried oregano
1 tablespoon crumbled dried basil

1. In a large skillet, warm the olive oil over medium heat, then add the onions and cook, stirring a few times, until softened, about 5 minutes. Add the garlic and cook for 1 minute. Add the beef and cook, breaking it up into smaller pieces, until the meat is no longer pink. Season lightly with salt and pepper.

2. Scrape the contents of the skillet into the slow cooker. Add the tomato sauce and stir to combine. Cover and cook on LOW for 8 to 9 hours. Halfway through cooking, add the oregano and basil.

3. Serve the sauce hot over cooked pasta, or cool to room temperature and freeze in batches. The sauce will keep in the refrigerator for up to 5 days and in the freezer for up to 3 months.

Lots-o'-Garlic Sauce for Stuffed Pasta

his is a lovely, homey tomato sauce for tortellini, tortelloni, agnolotti, or ravioli. Don't skip the little bit of honey.

⊙ Makes about 6 ½ cups, enough for 2 pounds pasta

COOKER: Medium round or oval
SETTING AND COOK TIME: LOW for 5 to 6 hours

7 cloves garlic, minced
3 tablespoons olive oil
One 28-ounce can whole plum tomatoes with their juice, chopped or
   crushed with your hands
One 6-ounce can tomato paste
One 15-ounce can tomato sauce
1 teaspoon crumbled dried basil
¼ teaspoon fennel seeds, crushed in a mortar
1 tablespoon honey
¼ cup dry red or white wine
Salt and freshly ground black pepper to taste

1. In a small skillet, slowly heat the garlic and olive oil together over medium heat until the garlic is softened, 1 to 2 minutes; do not let the garlic become brown or it will be bitter. Place the garlic, tomatoes, tomato paste, tomato sauce, basil, fennel, honey, and wine in the slow cooker and stir to combine. Cover and cook on LOW for 5 to 6 hours.

2. Season the sauce with salt and pepper. If not serving with hot pasta immediately, you can keep the sauce in the crock on KEEP WARM for a few hours. The sauce will keep, in a tightly covered container, in the refrigerator for up to 3 days or in the freezer for up to 2 months.

Crock Macaroni and Tillamook Cheese

I love old-fashioned pasta tubes in a rich, cheesy sauce. The combination of evaporated milk and the egg eliminates the need for flour as a thickening agent. Don't attempt this recipe without using the canned milk (you can use skim if you like); it stabilizes the sauce so it will not curdle as fresh-milk sauces do in the slow cooker. ○ *Serves 6*

COOKER: Medium or large round
SETTING AND COOK TIME: LOW for 3½ to 4 hours

8 ounces (about 2 heaping cups) whole-wheat penne
2 tablespoons unsalted butter, softened
¼ cup olive oil
1½ cups milk
One 12-ounce can evaporated milk
2 large eggs
One 8-ounce container sour cream
1 teaspoon salt
⅛ teaspoon cayenne pepper
3 cups (12 ounces) shredded Tillamook or other mild cheddar cheese
½ cup freshly grated or shredded Parmesan cheese

1. Parcook the pasta in boiling salted water until barely softened, about 5 minutes. Grease the bottom and sides of the crock with the softened butter. Drain the pasta and add the hot pasta to the crock. Stir in the olive oil.

2. In a medium-size bowl, combine both milks, the eggs, sour cream, salt, and cayenne and whisk until smooth. Add the cheddar, then pour the mixture over the pasta in the crock; gently stir with a rubber spatula to evenly coat the pasta. Sprinkle the Parmesan evenly over the top. Cover and cook on LOW for 3½ to 4 hours, until the custard is set in the center and the pasta is tender.

3. The pasta can remain in the slow cooker on KEEP WARM for 30 minutes. For a special touch, you can sauté some fresh bread crumbs in butter or olive oil and sprinkle over the pasta before serving.

Turkey Chili Mac

Some people just go crazy for chili mac. You can leave out the corn and olives if you like yours plain, but they make this really tasty. ○ *Serves 6*

COOKER: Medium or large round or oval
SETTING AND COOK TIME: LOW for 5 to 5½ hours; pasta, corn, and olives added at 4 hours

1 tablespoon olive oil
1 small yellow onion, finely chopped
1 clove garlic, minced
1 pound ground dark turkey
One 14.5-ounce can diced tomatoes, drained
2½ teaspoons good-quality chili powder
½ teaspoon ancho chile powder
Pinch of ground cumin
Pinch of crumbled dried marjoram
½ teaspoon salt
8 ounces (about 2 heaping cups) elbow macaroni, baby shells, or mini penne, parcooked in
　　boiling salted water for 5 minutes and drained
½ cup frozen baby white corn, thawed
One 2-ounce can sliced black olives, drained
1 to 2 cups (4 to 8 ounces) shredded white or yellow cheddar cheese, to your taste
¼ cup chopped fresh cilantro, for serving

1. Coat the inside of the crock with nonstick cooking spray.

2. In a medium-size skillet, heat the olive oil over medium-high heat, then add the onion and garlic and cook, stirring a few times, until softened, about 5 minutes; stir in the ground turkey. Cook until the turkey is cooked through, stirring occasionally to break it up into smaller pieces. Drain the fat from the pan, then transfer the turkey to the crock. Add the tomatoes, chili and chile powders, cumin, marjoram, and salt; stir to combine. Cover and cook on LOW for 4 hours.

3. Stir the warm parcooked pasta, the corn, and the olives into the chili. Cover and cook on LOW for another 1 to 1½ hours.

4. Top with the cheese and let it melt, then serve the chili mac right out of the crock, or sprinkle the cheese over individual portions, along with the cilantro.

Slow Cooker Polenta

Making polenta has never been this simple. Polenta by itself is bland, so it likes to be dressed up with toppings of cheese, herbs, or a marinara sauce. I love to serve it sprinkled with both Parmesan and fontina cheeses. If doubling or tripling the recipe for a group, be sure to use a large slow cooker; the mixture should never fill the crock more than three-quarters full. Please note the higher water-to-grain ratio needed in the slow cooker; it is 5 to 1 instead of the 4 to 1 in traditionally prepared polenta recipes. ○ *Serves 8*

COOKER: Medium or large round or oval
SETTINGS AND COOK TIMES: HIGH for 30 minutes, then LOW for about 5 hours

7½ cups water
1½ cups coarse-grain yellow polenta
1½ teaspoons salt
½ cup (1 stick) unsalted butter, for serving (optional)
1 cup (4 ounces) freshly grated Parmesan or shredded Italian fontina cheese, for serving (optional)

1. Place the water, polenta, and salt in the slow cooker. Whisk for a few seconds. Cover and cook on HIGH for 30 minutes.

2. Stir again, set the cooker to LOW, and cook for 5 hours, stirring occasionally with a wooden spoon. The polenta will thicken quite quickly after 2 hours, expanding magically in the cooker and looking like it is done, but it will need the extra time to cook all the grains evenly.

3. At 5 hours, taste and make sure the desired consistency has been reached and the grains are tender throughout. The longer the polenta cooks, the creamier it will become. When done, it will be smooth and very thick yet pourable, and a wooden spoon will stand up in the polenta without falling over (the true test). The cooked polenta can sit in the cooker on LOW for up to 1 hour before serving; add a bit of hot water if it gets too stiff. Stir before serving.

4. To serve, use an oversize spoon to portion some polenta onto a plate or into a shallow soup bowl. Top with a pat of butter and sprinkle with the cheese, if using, or top the polenta with a stew or braised meat with lots of sauce. Serve immediately.

Creamed Corn and Parmesan Risotto

T his is a luscious year-round risotto. You can leave out the wine and replace it with another cup of broth if you like. This is also good served with some chopped fresh chives sprinkled on top. Serve with a big green salad. ● *Serves 4 to 6*

COOKER: Large round
SETTING AND COOK TIME: HIGH for 2½ hours; corn added at 1½ hours

3 tablespoons olive oil
1 large onion, finely chopped
2 cups (12 ounces) raw Arborio rice
½ cup white wine or Prosecco
6 cups (one 48-ounce can) low-sodium chicken broth or light vegetable broth, heated
One 15-ounce can creamed corn
1½ cups frozen baby white corn kernels, thawed
½ cup heavy cream or plain soy milk
2 tablespoons unsalted butter
Salt and freshly ground black pepper to taste
¾ cup freshly grated Parmesan cheese, plus more for serving
3 plum tomatoes (optional), seeded and chopped, for topping

1. In a medium-size skillet over medium heat, warm the oil. Add the onion and cook until softened, about 5 minutes, stirring a few times. Add the rice and cook for a few minutes, stirring occasionally, until it turns chalky and is coated with the oil. Add the wine and bring to a boil, then reduce the heat to medium-low and simmer for 2 minutes. Using a heatproof rubber spatula, scrape everything into the slow cooker. Add the hot broth. Cover and cook on HIGH for 1½ hours.

2. Stir in the creamed corn and corn kernels; cover quickly and cook for another hour. When done, the risotto should be creamy and tender but still slightly firm in the center.

3. Add the cream and butter and season with salt and pepper. Cover and wait 1 minute for the butter to soften. Uncover and stir in the cheese. The risotto can sit in the cooker on KEEP WARM for up to 1 hour before serving. Serve, spooned into bowls, with additional Parmesan for sprinkling. Pass a bowl with the diced tomatoes, if using, for topping.

Risotto with Zucchini and Peas

While Italy is synonymous with pasta, culinarily speaking, Italians in the northern provinces of the country are mainly rice eaters. They eat not just steamed rice, but a uniquely prepared rice dish that is braised, called risotto. As with all braises, the slow cooker excels at this once time-consuming task. For risotto, only a short-grain rice will do. There are three risotto rices: Arborio rice, grown in northern Italy, makes for a sticky risotto. Vialone nano has more body and is the risotto rice of choice in Venice and Verona. Carnaroli is another Italian rice used for risotto; it is now also grown in Argentina. ○ *Serves 4 to 6*

COOKER: Large round
SETTING AND COOK TIME: HIGH for 2½ hours; zucchini and peas added at 2 hours

5 tablespoons unsalted butter

1 medium-size onion, finely chopped

2 cups (12 ounces) raw Arborio rice

½ cup white wine

6 cups (one 48-ounce can) low-sodium chicken broth or light vegetable broth, heated

2 tablespoons olive oil

1 pound zucchini, cut into ½-inch cubes

2 cups frozen petite peas, thawed

Salt and freshly ground black pepper to taste

¾ cup freshly grated Parmesan cheese, plus more for serving

1. In a medium-size skillet over medium heat, heat 3 tablespoons of the butter until sizzling. Add the onion and cook until softened, about 5 minutes, stirring a few times. Add the rice, stirring occasionally, for a few minutes, until it turns chalky and is coated with the oil. Add the wine and bring to a boil, then reduce the heat to medium-low and simmer for 2 minutes. Using a heatproof rubber spatula, scrape everything into the slow cooker. Add the hot broth. Cover and cook on HIGH for 2 hours.

2. While the risotto is cooking, in a small skillet, warm the olive oil. Add the zucchini and cook over medium-high heat until just soft and a bit golden around the edges, stirring a few times. Don't cook completely, as it's going to cook more along with the risotto in the crock. Set aside.

3. At 2 hours, stir in the zucchini and peas; cover quickly. Cover and cook for another 30 minutes. When done, the risotto should be creamy and tender but still slightly firm in the center. The vegetables will still be bright green.

4. Add the remaining 2 tablespoons butter and season with salt and pepper. Cover and wait 1 minute for the butter to soften. Uncover and stir in the cheese. The risotto can sit in the cooker on KEEP WARM for up to 1 hour before serving. Serve, spooned into bowls, with additional Parmesan for sprinkling.

Slow Cooker Tip: LOW Maintenance Slow-Cooking

If you are leaving the slow cooker unattended during the day or cooking overnight, it is best to cook on the LOW setting. That way, there is no chance your food will overcook or burn. Most pot roasts, soups, chilis, and stews cook best on the LOW setting anyway.

Mexican Rice and Beans with Cheese

I n Mexican cooking, a medium-grain white rice is used in *sopas secas* (dry soups), which are like thick stews. Converted rice is a perfect substitute here. This rice casserole is loaded with cottage cheese and beans for tasty protein. I like to serve this with fresh corn on the cob and a sprinkle of cilantro. ○ *Serves 4 to 6*

COOKER: Medium round or oval
SETTING AND COOK TIME: LOW for 7 to 8 hours

1½ cups raw converted rice
One 14.5-ounce can fire-roasted diced tomatoes with their juice
One 16-ounce can pinto beans, undrained
2 cloves garlic, minced
1 medium-size onion, finely chopped
2 tablespoons light olive oil
1 cup (8 ounces) small-curd cottage cheese
One 4-ounce can diced roasted green chiles, drained
2 cups (8 ounces) shredded Monterey Jack cheese

1. Coat the inside of the crock with olive oil nonstick cooking spray. Combine the rice, tomatoes, beans, garlic, onion, olive oil, cottage cheese, chiles, and 1 cup of the shredded cheese in the slow cooker; stir with a rubber spatula to mix evenly. Cover and cook on LOW for 7 to 8 hours, until the rice is tender.

2. Just before serving, sprinkle with the remaining 1 cup shredded cheese, cover, and let stand for 10 minutes to melt the cheese. Spoon out of the crock to serve.

Chicken and Shrimp Jambalaya

J ambalaya is a complex-tasting one-pot dish, composed of rice, onions, green peppers, tomatoes, and a protein, such as ham or bacon, poultry, shellfish, or any combination thereof. Cajun seasoning is a spice blend that's now easy to find in supermarkets. ○ *Serves 4*

COOKER: Medium or large round or oval
SETTING AND COOK TIME: LOW for 5 to 6 hours, or HIGH for 2½ to 3 hours;
  then 10 to 15 minutes on HIGH to cook the shrimp

1 large yellow onion, chopped
1 cup thinly sliced celery
One 14.5-ounce can low-sodium diced tomatoes with their juice
One 14.5-ounce can low-sodium chicken broth
⅓ cup tomato paste (half of a 6-ounce can)
1½ tablespoons Worcestershire sauce
1½ teaspoons Cajun seasoning
1 pound skinless, boneless skinless chicken breast halves or thighs, trimmed of fat and
    cut into ¾-inch pieces
1½ cups raw converted rice
8 ounces large shrimp (16/20 or 23/30 count), peeled and deveined
¾ cup chopped green bell pepper

1. Coat the inside of the crock with nonstick cooking spray. Combine the onion, celery, tomatoes, broth, tomato paste, Worcestershire sauce, and Cajun seasoning in the crock. Stir in the chicken and rice. Cover and cook on LOW for 5 to 6 hours or HIGH for 2½ to 3 hours, until most of the liquid is absorbed, the chicken is cooked through, and the rice is tender.

2. Stir in the shrimp and bell pepper. Set the cooker to HIGH (if it's not already), cover, and let stand for 10 to 15 minutes, until the shrimp are pink and firm. Serve immediately in shallow bowls with fresh French bread and butter.

Char Siu Pork Fried Rice

I n the Chinese kitchen, pork is the red meat of choice for its clean, light taste and versatility. Char siu is a Chinese version of barbecue; the marinade gives a haunting sweetness to the meat. It is the traditional ingredient in fried rice and steamed buns. Fried rice is usually a stovetop dish, but imagine my surprise when I found out it could also be made in the slow cooker. Fried rice was invented for leftover cooked rice. If you don't have any cold cooked rice on hand, go ahead and make a fresh batch of rice, spread it in a single layer on a baking sheet, and let it cool to room temperature. Place the uncovered baking sheet in the refrigerator and chill for at least 1 hour, or overnight, before using. (I've used fresh-cooked rice that has been chilled for an hour and it worked fine in this recipe; you want the rice to harden a bit.) The Char Siu Pork takes 2 hours to marinate and 8 hours to cook, so make it the day before you plan to serve the pork fried rice. **o** *Serves 4*

COOKER: Large oval

SETTINGS AND COOK TIMES: Pork, LOW for 8 hours; Rice, HIGH for 1½ hours, green onions and salt added after 1 hour

6 cups cold leftover cooked rice (white or brown rice, long-, medium- or short-grain, as desired), left to stand at room temperature 30 minutes before assembling dish

1½ cups finely diced cooked Char Siu Pork (page 242)

1 cup frozen petite peas, thawed

½ cup diced or shredded carrot, bell pepper, or celery, or a combination

3 baby bok choy, cut across into ¼-inch-wide ribbons, or
    ½ cup shredded napa cabbage

2 dried shiitake mushrooms, soaked in hot water for 20 minutes, drained, and thinly sliced

4 large eggs

1 teaspoon Thai-style hot chili sauce

2 teaspoons peeled and finely minced or grated fresh ginger

6 green onions (white part and some of the green), thinly sliced

1 teaspoon salt, or to taste, or 3 to 4 tablespoons low-sodium soy sauce or tamari

1. Coat the inside of the crock with nonstick cooking spray twice or brush it with sesame oil.

2. Combine the rice, diced pork, peas, carrot, bok choy, and mushrooms in a large bowl. Break the eggs into a cup or small bowl, add the chili sauce, and beat gently with a fork. Pour the eggs into the crock and sprinkle with the ginger. Place the rice mixture on top of the eggs, taking care not to splash the eggs; *do not stir.* Cover and cook on HIGH for 1 hour, allowing the rice to heat up and grow fragrant. The eggs will set on the bottom like an omelet.

3. With a plastic rice paddle or heat-resistant rubber spatula, stir the rice from the bottom to the top, folding the rice and eggs over and over to distribute the egg bits as evenly as possible throughout the rice. Add the green onions, then the salt or soy sauce (don't use soy sauce if you want the rice to stay white). Cover and cook on HIGH for 30 minutes longer, until nice and hot. Serve immediately.

Char Siu Pork

¼ cup hoisin sauce

¼ cup low-sodium soy sauce

3 tablespoons ketchup

3 tablespoons honey

2 tablespoons Shaoxing wine (Chinese rice wine) or dry sherry

1 clove garlic, pressed

Two 2-inch pieces fresh ginger, peeled and grated

½ teaspoon Chinese five-spice powder or 1 star anise with points broken off

One 2-pound boneless Boston butt pork roast, trimmed of excess fat

1. In a small bowl, combine the hoisin sauce, soy sauce, ketchup, honey, wine, garlic, ginger, and five-spice powder; stir until smooth. Place the mixture in a large zipper-top plastic bag. Add the pork roast to the bag, and turn to coat the pork with the marinade. Allow the pork to marinate in the refrigerator for at least 2 hours, or up to overnight.

2. Coat the inside of the crock with nonstick cooking spray. Place the pork and the marinade in the crock. Cover and cook on LOW for 8 hours.

3. Remove the pork from the crock using a slotted spoon; place the roast on a cutting board or clean work surface and cover with aluminum foil. You can dice the pork and use it in Char Siu Pork Fried Rice, or serve the roast sliced with rice and steamed vegetables. If you want a bit of sauce, add 1 cup chicken broth to the glaze in the crock after removing the meat; stir well. Drizzle the sauce over the meat when serving.

Easiest Ever Rice and Vegetables

Sometimes all I want for lunch is something that's completely easy to put together in the slow cooker, and this recipe certainly fits the bill. I can get broth from the cupboard and clean out the veggie drawer. You can also mix in thawed frozen vegetables, like artichoke hearts, peas, or green pepper strips. Each time I make this, I use a different combination of vegetables, and no two batches are the same. Be sure to slice, chop, or dice all of the vegetables a uniform size to insure that everything cooks evenly. ○ *Serves 4*

COOKER: Medium round or oval
SETTING AND COOK TIME: HIGH for 2 hours

1½ cups raw converted rice
¼ teaspoon seasoning of your choice, such as lemon pepper, a mixed salt-free seasoning such
    as Spike, or a dash of chili powder or smoked paprika
2 to 2½ cups mixed vegetables, such as sliced celery, peas, edamame, baby limas, bell pepper
    strips, sliced artichoke hearts, small cauliflower florets, sliced mushrooms, green beans,
    sliced carrots, sliced zucchini, and chopped fresh spinach, tough stems removed
1 tablespoon olive oil
One 14.5-ounce can low-sodium chicken broth or light vegetable broth, heated until very hot
¾ cup boiling water
3 green onions (white part and some of the green), chopped, *or* 3 tablespoons chopped fresh
    chives, Italian parsley, or cilantro, for sprinkling

1. Coat the inside of the crock with olive oil nonstick cooking spray. Place the rice in the crock and sprinkle with the seasoning. Add the vegetables, olive oil, hot broth, and boiling water; stir to combine. Cover and cook on HIGH for about 2 hours, until the liquid is absorbed, the vegetables are cooked through, and the rice is tender.

2. Serve immediately in shallow bowls topped with the green onions, along with fresh French bread, toasted country bread, or warm flour tortillas and butter.

Measurement Equivalents

Please note that all conversions are approximate.

Liquid Conversions

U.S.	Metric	U.S.	Metric
1 tsp	5 ml	1 cup	240 ml
1 tbs	15 ml	1 cup + 2 tbs	275 ml
2 tbs	30 ml	1¼ cups	300 ml
3 tbs	45 ml	1⅓ cups	325 ml
¼ cup	60 ml	1½ cups	350 ml
⅓ cup	75 ml	1⅔ cups	375 ml
⅓ cup + 1 tbs	90 ml	1¾ cups	400 ml
⅓ cup + 2 tbs	100 ml	1¾ cups + 2 tbs	450 ml
½ cup	120 ml	2 cups (1 pint)	475 ml
⅔ cup	150 ml	2½ cups	600 ml
¾ cup	180 ml	3 cups	720 ml
¾ cup + 2 tbs	200 ml	4 cups (1 quart)	945 ml

(1,000 ml is 1 liter)

Weight Conversions

U.S. / U.K.	Metric	U.S. / U.K.	Metric
½ oz	14 g	7 oz	200 g
1 oz	28 g	8 oz	227 g
1½ oz	43 g	9 oz	255 g
2 oz	57 g	10 oz	284 g
2½ oz	71 g	11 oz	312 g
3 oz	85 g	12 oz	340 g
3½ oz	100 g	13 oz	368 g
4 oz	113 g	14 oz	400 g
5 oz	142 g	15 oz	425 g
6 oz	170 g	1 lb	454 g

Oven Temperature Conversions

°F	Gas Mark	°C
250	½	120
275	1	140
300	2	150
325	3	165
350	4	180
375	5	190
400	6	200
425	7	220
450	8	230
475	9	240
500	10	260
550	Broil	290

Index

With the Not Your Mother's® Cookbooks, Dinner Is Served!

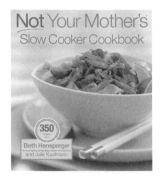

Not Your Mother's Slow Cooker Cookbook

"From meatloaf to soups to desserts, this book might make your oven a storage space . . . The perfect companion to a Crock-Pot." —*Boston Herald*

"One of the best . . . a compilation of recipes that is thoroughly modern, covering a wide flavor spectrum." —*Times Union*

". . . gives slow cooking a hip new twist." —*Slow Cooking* (*Woman's Day* special publication)

Not Your Mother's Slow Cooker Recipes for Two

"Great gift for singles and small families who want the convenience of a small slow-cooker-made meal without sacrificing wholesomeness and flavor." —*Orlando Sentinel*

"The recipes are fresh and sophisticated." —*Ann Arbor News*

"Recipes call for fresh ingredients and cater to modern tastes and nutrition concerns . . . [Gives] the single diner or a hungry twosome reason to forget takeout and really enjoy a home-cooked dinner without unwelcome after-work hassle." —*San Francisco Chronicle*

Not Your Mother's Slow Cooker Recipes for Entertaining

". . . Can help you serve a great meal, even if you're an occasional cook." —*Los Angeles Daily News*

". . . [coaxes] more ambitious food from the Rodney Dangerfield of appliances . . . Entrees rise above the usual chilis and stews, with non–slow cooker recipes for complementary side dishes and salads." —*Washington Post*

Not Your Mother's Weeknight Cooking

"This is a good cookbook to help you get through the workweek, especially if you're regularly pressed for time and short on creativity." —*Richmond Times-Dispatch*

"*Not Your Mother's Weeknight Cooking* features 150 delicious recipes that your family will love and you will feel good about serving, with dozens of options for tasty meals every day of the week." —*Treasure Valley Family Magazine*

"Those excuses like 'it's too many ingredients' or 'it'll take all night to make' evaporate when you open *Not Your Mother's Weeknight Cooking* . . . Most dishes would make a nutritionist proud—and your dining companions happy." —*Washington Post Express*